TRAVEL TO CHINA

EVERYTHING YOU NEED TO KNOW BEFORE YOU GO

JOSH SUMMERS

travelchinacheaper

Edited by: Leeanne Hendrick
Layout: Genessa Neeser

Some of the links in this book represent affiliations with 3rd party companies. The author of this book may be compensated should you choose to use the services mentioned therein.

ISBN-13: 978-1-7321204-1-9
IBSN-10: 1-7321204-1-2

Table of Contents

Introduction..1

Welcome to China

Should I Travel to China?......................................6

What to Expect...10

Solo Travel vs Tour Group..................................26

Getting a Visa to China

Applying for a Chinese Visa................................32

China Transit Visas..36

Beyond the Visa: Proper Registration..................43

China Visa FAQ..45

Preparing to Travel to China

Preparing for China...52

What Documents Do I Need?...............................53

What Vaccines Do I Need?...................................55

All About the Money...59

Planning Your Itinerary..65

Packing for China..69

Purchasing Your China Flights.............................73

Finding Accommodation in China

What to Expect with Chinese Hotels....................78

How to Find Good Hotels in China.......................82

What to Expect with Hostels in China..................86

Homestays and Camping in China.......................89

Transportation Within China

Guide to Flying in China..94
Guide to Taking a Train in China...........................99
Guide to Using Taxis in China 120
Guide to Taking a Bus in China 124
Guide to Renting a Car in China 134
Guide to Bike Rentals in China 137

Staying Connected in China

Setting up a Mobile Phone in China 140
Censorship & the Internet in China.......................143
Communicating Back Home from China 146
Sending & Receiving Mail in China 148

Navigating the Chinese Language Barrier

The Chinese Language(s) 152
How to Travel China without Learning Chinese....155
Learning Chinese Before You Go 160
Ordering at a Chinese Restaurant........................ 164

Staying Healthy in China

What to Expect at a Chinese Hospital.................. 170
Do I Need Travel Insurance?.................................172
Traveling in China with Disabilities 176

Frequently Asked Questions...............................177

Appendix 181

Dedicated to my incredible travel companions:
my wife Tiffany
and my sons Jaden and Josiah.

Introduction
Join me for Coffee?

Welcome! I'm excited that you've decided to make the first step in your trip to China by purchasing this guide. I genuinely hope you find this book to be useful as you plan your upcoming journey.

Before you start, I want to warn you about one very important thing: this is not a typical travel guide. I'm not trying to say that this guide is *special* or far superior to any other China guide on the market; it's just...different. How?

First, I'm *not* going to be telling you where to go and what places to see in China. As the old saying goes, I'd much rather teach you "how to fish" than to merely serve fish to you on a platter. Instead of listing all the places you need to visit when you're in Beijing (such as The Great Wall, the Summer Palace and the Temple of Heaven), I want to teach you how to properly navigate the public transportation that will get you there, how to get the cash you'll need to pay the entrance fee, and how to make sure you can communicate with people along the way.

We'll also take a step back from there and figure out how to make sure we get the right Chinese visa, pack your suitcase with everything you'll need and even find the best Chinese hotels that will meet your expectations.

> It's everything you need to know *before* you begin this journey bound for China.

Second important point: this isn't your normal travel guide because I've decided to make it much more personal. Imagine that you and I are good friends sitting together at a local coffee shop. I've just returned from a decade of traveling around China, and I want to prepare you as best as I can for your upcoming trip and answer all of your most pressing questions.

This guide is a conversation between you and I where we walk step-by-step through the process of traveling to China.

My goal is that by the time you finish this book, you'll not only be more excited for your trip, you'll also have the right expectations in mind and the tools to make the journey successful.

So, let's sit down together. I've ordered a hot, caramel macchiato - my favorite coffee beverage - and I'm eager to answer your questions about China. I'm glad that you're joining me!

- Josh Summers

WELCOME TO CHINA!

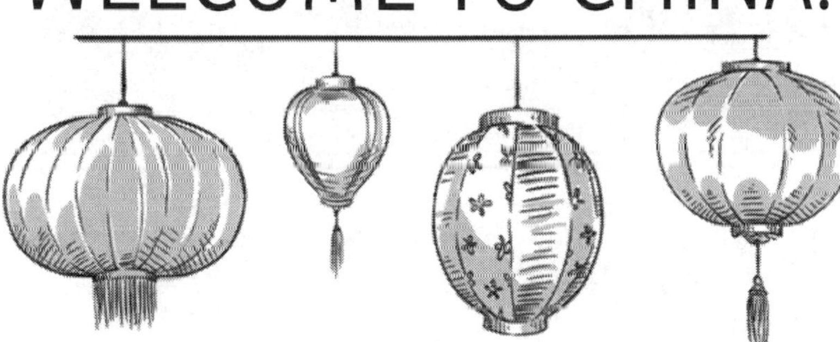

Should I Travel to China?

I realize that there are a number of travelers who buy this book who haven't quite decided whether or not they want to travel to China. If you're already set and determined to go, then you can skip this chapter.

If, however, you're still on the fence, I'd like to take a moment to share my thoughts on what attracts me to China. What makes this a country worth visiting? If travel is about broadening our horizons and cultural understanding, how does China fit into this?

The Benefits of Traveling to China

China is quick to tell anybody who will listen that the country has over 5,000 years of history. Of course, they don't have any basis for this claim[1] and historians note that we only have records that date back to China's Shang Dynasty in 1600 BC (which would bring us to only about 3,600 years of recorded history). But that's beside the point.

---

[1] https://camphorpress.com/5000-years-of-history/

The point is that China has a depth of history and culture that is almost unparalleled in the world today. There are more UNESCO World Heritage Sites in China (52) than there are in the United States, Australia and Israel...*combined!*[2]

China officially recognizes 55 different ethnic minority groups which make up almost 9% of the country's population. These minority groups represent many languages, religions, and cultural norms that look nothing like the "China" you might imagine.

> The benefit of traveling to and throughout China is the opportunity to experience this diversity in history, culture, and natural scenery first-hand.

Visiting China is different than visiting Europe or going on holiday to Australia. Unless you're being guided by a tour group the entire time, there's an element of adventure that frankly I've become addicted to while traveling around the country. You don't come here to relax on a beach, in my opinion. You come to China for the experiential memories.

If you're into history, China has plenty that will keep you interested. From the Great Wall and the Forbidden City in the east, to the Silk Road with all of its ancient cities and Buddhist caves in the west, it would be impossible to see it all in a single lifetime.

---

[2] https://en.wikipedia.org/wiki/World_Heritage_Sites_by_country

If you're into beautiful scenery, you should definitely keep your camera handy while traveling around China! Once outside the big, polluted cities, you'll come face-to-face with endless rice paddies, majestic mountain ranges, undulating desert sand dunes, and unique places that would make you feel like you're living the movie Avatar because, well, Avatar filmed some of its most breathtaking scenes in China![3]

If you love experiencing world cultures and different cuisines, China makes that quite easy as well. Almost every province in China has its own cultural idiosyncrasies or unique cuisine. This could be the difference between Opera in Beijing and the mask-changing Opera in Chengdu, the difference between Cantonese food in Guangdong and lamb-filled Uyghur food in Xinjiang, or the difference between the monasteries of Tibet and the mosques in Xi'an.

The (Unnecessary) Excuses

There are plenty of excuses I've heard for why people are too afraid to travel to China. These excuses include but are not limited to:

- *"I don't speak Chinese! I'll get lost or won't be able to read the signs."*
- *"There are just too many people!"*
- *"I'm used to a certain comfort level. I could never use a squatty toilet and what if the beds aren't comfortable?"*

---

[3] https://en.wikipedia.org/wiki/Zhangjiajie_National_Forest_Park

- *"I won't know what to eat. I can't do spicy food and I'm gluten intolerant."*

These are valid concerns, no doubt, but they aren't good excuses for avoiding China. I believe that the benefits of what you'll get by experiencing this country will far outweigh any trepidation or initial discomfort you'll feel when you first arrive.

In the next few pages, I want to help overcome the fears you might have by giving you a picture of what you can expect when you come to China. The more you understand, the easier it will be to make an informed decision about whether China is the right place for you to visit.

So...Should I Travel to China?

In the end, the decision is obviously only yours to make. I don't want to even attempt to make it for you! You should weigh the pros and cons: How much will it cost to travel to China? Do you prefer to sit on a beach during your vacation or check off amazing "I've been there!" sites from your bucket list?

Whatever the case may be, I guarantee China has the potential to meet and even exceed your expectations. *The key is to have your expectations appropriately set and to be properly prepared for the journey.* That's where the following chapters in this book will come in very handy for you.

What to Expect

Last year I guided two sets of travelers to a particular city in China. Almost everything about these two trips were identical: both groups were middle-income Americans, and we all visited the same locations. We stayed at the same hotels, and we ate pretty much the same food.

In the end, one of the groups loved the trip, and the other group complained. I was completely confused as to how this could be until I spoke with the members of the group that complained. I came to realize one very simple but important rule of travel: The success of any trip is often directly related to a traveler's willingness to assume realistic expectations.

> "The success of any trip is often directly related to a traveler's willingness to assume realistic expectations."

The travelers in the second group were expecting something completely different than what they experienced when they landed in China. These differences led to the inevitable feeling of disappointment.

Because of this, I'd like to spend a little time helping you understand what you *should* expect when you travel to China. In some cases, this may not align with what you were originally anticipating, and that's okay. It could be that you just have no idea what to expect. Either way, I want to make things as clear as I can for you.

What to Expect · Weather

Once you understand how big China is, you'll quickly realize that determining the weather in China depends entirely on where you'll be in the country. I recommend you do a bit of research on the specific cities you hope to visit. To do this, you can either Google "historical weather for ______" or you can visit the following website to explore climate averages for each city in China:

www.timeanddate.com/weather/china

In general, the summer season (July-August) are quite hot all across the country. It's not the heat that makes it difficult though; it's the humidity in places along the eastern coast such as Beijing and Shanghai. Don't avoid traveling during these months but prepare accordingly. In places of high elevation (i.e. Tibet, Qinghai, etc.), be sure to bring sunscreen to protect yourself from the fierce sun, and no matter where you are, drink plenty of water. Thankfully, inexpensive bottles of purified water can be bought everywhere you go.

The winter months, which usually last from mid-November to March, provide the most diversity in climate. Places further north, such as Xinjiang, Inner Mongolia, and Heilongjiang (home to the famous Harbin ice festival) are bitter cold.

However, visiting the beaches of Sanya or walking around many parts of southern China are quite pleasant. If you're traveling during the winter, and you'll be hitting both northern and southern cities (such as going to both Beijing in the north and Hong Kong in the south), you'll have to pack both warm and cold weather clothing.

The majority of travelers tend to book travel to China during the lovely fall and spring months. This usually means March-June and September to mid-November for most regions around China.

Obviously, there are still extremes, so you'll still want to do research on your specific destinations. Most of the time, however, you won't need to plan for too much variance in climate. Keep in mind that you'll also be traveling with larger crowds during these periods, but that's the tradeoff.

What to Expect · Toilets

It's natural to be concerned about the toilets in China. Are there plenty of public toilets? Are they clean? *Do I have to use a squatty potty?!*

Let me put your mind at ease: China has come a *long way* over the past decade regarding the availability and sanitation of toilets. What you may have heard from past travelers or seen on film probably isn't what you'll experience when you arrive. A public toilet is still often a dirty public toilet, as it is anywhere in the world, but China may surprise you.

Most travelers spend weeks in China and never once have to use a squatty potty. Almost all hotels, major restaurants, and even train cars offer Western toilets. All of the major tourist attractions that you read about in travel guides will offer relatively clean, Western-style toilets. As long as you're staying within the major cities of China and not venturing too far into the countryside, you'll more than likely have consistent access to clean, Western-style toilets.

The trouble only comes when you start getting off the beaten path. I've taken buses into remote parts of western China where the "pit stop" was the bus literally stopping on the side of the road and finding privacy behind a big rock. Of course, this was an *extremely* remote part of the country, and I knew going into it that the toilet situation would be different. If you'll be going somewhere off the beaten path, any good tour guide or guide book will let you know what to expect with the toilets.

Don't let the toilets scare you. Most people end their travels in China having never had to worry once about availability, comfort, or cleanliness.

Important Note: While public toilets are readily available throughout China's major cities and tourist attractions, toilet paper and hand soap often are not. I recommend you always bring along a travel bottle of hand sanitizer and a pack of tissue paper in your day bag.

What to Expect · Pollution

When it comes to air quality, China has earned a pretty bad reputation. There are times when I don't even allow my sons to play outside because my wife and I are worried about the pollution in the air. Thankfully, new regulations and policies mean that it's getting better, but it's still going to be a decade or more before noticeable improvement is seen.

Pollution in the air is measured on a scale known as the Air Quality Index, or "AQI" for short. It's an internationally accepted means of measuring the concentration of various pollutants over a period of time. Most AQI scales measure from 1-500, with one being amazingly clean air and 500 being dangerously polluted.

Whereas most cities in the United States and Europe maintain a measurement under AQI 50, it's quite common to see an AQI 150 or more for Chinese cities on average.

So, how does this affect your travels and what can you do? First, recognize that pollution is a reality that you'll have to face in China, and the truth is that exposure during a short trip is likely not going to have long-term health effects. Second, if you're worried about pollution, buy a cheap pollution mask before you leave and wear it anytime the pollution gets above AQI 100.

Many people who live in China, including myself, keep an app on their phone that gives you up-to-the-hour AQI measurements to check throughout the day. One of the most popular apps is Air Matters, which happens to also be free for both iTunes and Google Play:

- Air Matters (iTunes): www.travelchinacheaper.com/air-matters-itunes
- Air Matters (Google Play): www.travelchinacheaper.com/air-matters-googleplay

What to Expect · Hotels

I'll go into much more detail about what you can expect while staying at a Chinese Hotel later, but I'd like to briefly address common fears I hear about hotels in China.

Like any country, there are good hotels in China, and there are bad hotels. The same goes for hostels. By law, foreign travelers are supposed to stay in hotels that are rated three-star or greater, but this isn't always enforced.

To make matters a bit more complicated, the Chinese hotel rating system doesn't always align with international standards, meaning that a four- or five-star hotel in China may not look like a four- or five-star hotel in the USA or Europe.

All that being said, most hotels and hostels in China offer more than enough comfort to make any fears you might have unnecessary. I've never been in a hotel that doesn't have a Western toilet. Almost every hotel offers a TV and internet connection nowadays, although you shouldn't expect to find any English channels, and the speed of the internet may
not be fast.

For three-star hotels and lower, the bed might be a bit harder than you're used to and there have been times I haven't had hot water. However, in my experience the four- and five-star hotels provide very comfortable beds and reliable hot water.

If you're extremely worried about comfort, sticking with names such as Hilton, Sheraton, Radisson, and other international brands is guaranteed to keep you happy.

What to Expect · Transportation

Over the past decade, China has built an unbelievable system of public transportation. Whether it's subway lines, high-speed trains, or airplanes, you might be surprised at how much *more* efficient transportation is in China than your home country.

Trains and subways run on a schedule that rarely fall behind while flights in China are notoriously delayed.

You'll find more detailed guides to transportation in a later chapter, but for now I'll make note that from a comfort perspective, if you stick to high speed trains, airplanes, subways and taxis, you'll be reasonably satisfied. City buses can be confusing to the average traveler, but they can still be comfortable.

It's the long-distance buses that require careful consideration. While China has invested heavily in its rail system, the buses have received very little funding over the years. Long-distance buses in China are usually quite old, and in my experience as a tall American, not very comfortable.

They are an adventure, however, and one that you may not have a choice to make if you're headed to a place not serviced by a train.

What to Expect · Cost of Travel

Most people think of Asia - Southeast Asia in particular - as a low-cost holiday destination. For the most part, I would agree with this.

The challenge in estimating cost of travel is both the size of China and the various standards defining what "budget" is. The difference between the cost of travel in Beijing compared to the cost of travel in a smaller region like Gansu is night and day. Hotels, food, and taxis are all priced differently depending on the region. Likewise, what you may consider expensive might be a drop in the bucket for another traveler.

I'm a firm believer that it's possible to travel anywhere within the budget you set. Perhaps you'll need to compromise on a few luxury items or bunk up with seven other travelers in a cheap hostel bed, but it's possible. On the other hand, you may be surprised to find that your budget will carry you further than you thought.

There are a few costs that remain consistent throughout China. For example, domestic flights are priced at rates similar to what you'd find in other countries and they fluctuate wildly just like they would elsewhere in the world. On the other hand, train tickets in China don't fluctuate at all and trains are consistently one of the cheapest ways to get from one place to another.

Oh, yeah, and a cup of Starbucks coffee is still the equivalent of US$6, so don't think you'll get any sort of discount there!

What to Expect · Local Customs & Etiquette

China offers an interesting contrast for travelers who come from the Western world. The etiquette that we value - things such as chewing with our mouth closed, standing in line, not spitting in public, not staring at people and not asking inappropriate questions like how much your salary is back home - are not the things that the Chinese value.

This may come as a shock to first-time visitors of China, but for those of us that live here it quickly becomes normal. While you may not have the luxury of time to normalize this different set of local customs, you can arm yourself with a good attitude and open mind. When somebody cuts in front of you in line, try not to get mad. Understand that in a country of 1.6 billion people, it sometimes takes a shameless attitude to get ahead.

Aside from expecting the unexpected behavior once you enter China, there are a few specific situations where an understanding of local customs and etiquette might come in handy. Because we are visitors to the country, Chinese people are usually quite understanding when we don't abide by their rules of etiquette, but they take notice when we do. Consider the following:

- **Respecting Your Elders**: In Chinese culture, elders are held in much higher esteem than they are in the Western world. It is customary to give up your seat to elders, allow elders to enter or exit a door before you, and care for whatever needs they might have.
- **At a Restaurant**: It is impolite to leave your chopsticks sticking straight up out of your rice bowl, as tempting as that may be. Also, don't be afraid to ask for a fork if you don't feel comfortable using chopsticks.
- **When Visiting a Local Home**: It is impolite to arrive at any home without a gift. This gift doesn't have to be lavish - many times it is as simple as a bag of fruits that you bought down the street - but it does show respect for the host. If you're visiting a close family friend or somebody for whom you want to show extra honor, bringing a gift from your home country is an excellent idea. Also, once you arrive at a local home, remember to take off your shoes before entering. The host will more than likely offer you slippers as a reminder to do so.
- **If You're Given a Gift**: Politely refuse the gift, at least the first one or two times it is offered. If the gift is wrapped, local etiquette dictates that you should wait to open the gift unless the giver expressly asks you to open it.
- **If Attending a Wedding**: As much as Westerners cringe at the idea of giving cash instead of a thoughtful gift, in Chinese culture it is quite the opposite. Cash is the preferred gift for the bride and groom and the amount can range from 100-1,000 RMB (or more) depending on

how close your relationship is with the couple and your perceived level of wealth.

- **Tipping**: As a traveler, it feels awkward not to tip, and yet 90% of the time that's the local custom in China. You don't tip waitresses at restaurants, bellhops at hotels, taxi drivers, airport or train attendants. You can try, but usually they'll give you the money back. It's only at high-end restaurants, often the ones that cater to tourists, where you'll be given the option to tip. Even then, scan your check carefully to make sure that a "service fee" hasn't already been applied to your total.

What to Expect · Cuisine (Food)

One of my favorite parts of traveling around China is the diverse cuisine options. Almost every province of China boasts its own special food, and many have their own designated cuisine, such as Sichuan food, Cantonese food, Xinjiang food and more. As you've probably guessed, the Chinese food you get at a restaurant in the West is very different than the *real* Chinese food you're going to run into when you're physically in the country.

There are entire books written on the diversity of Chinese food, and I don't want to even pretend to replicate that sort of detailed explanation here. Instead, I'd like to separate China into five particular food groups, sharing with you what to expect and what you should definitely try.

- **Beijing and the Northeast**: Because rice is grown in southern China, northeast China has a cuisine that is traditionally more bread and noodle based. While traveling around Beijing, you'll notice quite a few restaurants that offer Beijing duck as well as something known as hot pot. Both are delicious and worth a try. Hot pot is a dish that is shared at a table where various meats and vegetables are stirred into a boiling pot of broth (sometimes plain, sometimes spicy), and eaten straight from the pot once cooked.
- **Sichuan and Central China**: Most people hear Sichuan food and immediately think "spicy", but that's not always true. While peppers are often added to Sichuan food, it is best known for its infusion of flavor into every dish. Popular dishes include Mapo Dofu (hot and spicy tofu), Dandan noodles and dry-fried green beans, although there are many, many more. The Sichuan dish that almost every traveler loves is GongBao JiDing, or what I describe as the "original and better tasting Kung Pao Chicken".
- **Xinjiang Cuisine**: I consider this place my second home, so I'm quite biased toward Xinjiang food! The cuisine is heavily influenced by the Uyghur and Hui ethnic groups who make up almost half of the population in Xinjiang, and includes lots of lamb, noodles, and the use of cumin and other spices. Popular dishes you should try include Polo, which is a type of rice pilaf, laghman, which is a local noodle dish, and DaPanJi, which translates to "A

big plate of chicken". This dish is pretty much exactly what it sounds like, and it is delicious.

- **Shanghai and the East Coast**: Throughout Shanghai and the east coast, seafood naturally dominates the menu along with lots of different steamed breads and dumplings. Shanghai is also known for adding a bit more sweetness to its dishes. Popular foods include stinky tofu, the jianbing street food, steamed crab, and various kinds of fish. There's plenty to explore within this east coast cuisine, so have fun with it!
- **Cantonese and the South**: Most people have heard of Cantonese food and are familiar with the famous Dim Sum dishes. What they don't know is that this region is known for cooking almost any and every kind of meat: snake, snail, duck tongue, etc. Eat cautiously! While Cantonese cuisine includes a good portion of seafood and dumplings similar to Shanghai and the east coast, it's best known for dishes like Sweet and Sour Pork, fried rice, and Chow mein.

What to Expect · Chinese Holidays

If you happen to travel to China during the months of January, February, May or October, there's a chance that you'll experience one of China's three major holidays: Spring Festival, May Holiday and National Day.

During these holidays, all transportation around China is booked, and tourist destinations are packed full of tourists. I'm not saying you shouldn't travel during these holidays, merely that you should expect lots of crowds and difficulty buying tickets. Let's look at these major holidays individually.

- **Spring Festival / Chinese New Year** (floating): The biggest holiday on the Chinese calendar is also a floating holiday, which means that the date changes each year. Usually, the New Year lands near the end of January or early February, and it will last a week. It's customary for Chinese people to return to their homes to celebrate with families, which means that millions upon millions of people migrate home, filling up all available trains and planes. Expect to hear relentless firecrackers and see lots of decorations on the street during this time. Many shops are also closed for the first few days of Spring Festival, so beware.
- **May Holiday** (May 1): While this holiday used to last for an entire week, the official government calendar only shows three days of national vacation now. The weather is great, so Chinese people still tend to make travel plans during this time.
- **National Day** (October 1-7): National Day celebrations are a time when China recognizes the anniversary of the republic's founding on October 1, 1949. There might be a parade in Beijing, but most of the time it's just a nice week off for the Chinese people. You can expect a mass of travelers but there aren't usually many festivities associated with National Day that you can witness.

There are quite a few other minor holidays scattered throughout the year, such as the Tomb Sweeping Festival in mid-April, the Dragon Boat Festival in mid-June, and the Mid-Autumn Festival in mid-September. When you factor in the holidays of specific ethnic groups throughout China, there are quite a few others that could be mentioned, but you'll want to check with local tourist companies to see if or how you can witness these festivities.

To find the date for this year's Chinese Spring Festival and other holidays, head over to:

www.travelchinacheaper.com/chinese-holidays

Solo Travel vs Tour Group

I remember my first visit to Xi'an's famous Terracotta Warriors back in 2007. My wife and I had joined a travel group since we still weren't completely comfortable traveling around on our own yet. The bus left our hostel early in the morning and drove an hour out of town.

As our vehicle came to a stop, I looked out the window expecting to see our final destination. Instead, we had pulled up to a silk factory, and our guide was telling us that we were taking a 20-minute break to understand how silk is made in China. While the exhibit was mildly interesting, it quickly became clear that this stop served one purpose only: we were brought here to shop and spend money.

We were tourists, and this was the proverbial trap.

As frustrating as these tourist traps are for most foreign travelers, it's important to remember that they are considered normal for Chinese tourists. In fact, I'd go so far as to say that it's expected when you are part of a Chinese tour group. Most Chinese tourists love these shopping detours!

While you may be predisposed to group travel or solo travel based on your own experience or budget, I hope you'll take a moment to understand the benefits of both. You might find that a mix of the two is the perfect recipe for your own China travel experience.

Benefits of Tour Group Travel

Most people I know join a tour group for one of two reasons:

1. They want somebody to take care of the itinerary and logistics for them;
2. They're unsure whether they can handle the language, transport, and culture on their own.

China is not solo-travel friendly, at least not in comparison to Europe or Southeast Asia. You need to have a strong sense of adventure and the flexibility to make mistakes when you travel alone.

Travel groups in China give you an opportunity to enjoy both the destination and the journey instead of focusing on how to get there, what you'll eat, what time everything closes, etc. You won't need to speak a lick of Mandarin Chinese (although learning a small bit is still helpful), and you won't have to research the history of each place you visit on your own.

The good news is that there are different kinds of tour groups you can join in China. There are informal groups you can sign up for at a hostel and others you can book months prior to your arrival. There are food tours, walking tours, history tours, and adventure tours.

If you're the kind of person who prefers to soak in the sights without the worry of logistics, you're obviously fit for a group tour. Even if you're like me and you appreciate the adventure of exploring on your own, there's a lot of historical and cultural context that a tour group can provide. Sure, you can walk through Beijing's Forbidden City and simply check that off your list of places you've seen, but you could also pay a few extra dollars to join a walking tour with a historian who can tell stories that will bring the halls of this palace to life for you.

If you'd like to learn more about the kinds of unique China tours that are available, I've listed some of my favorites in the appendix of this book.

Benefits of Solo Travel

On the other end of the travel spectrum, you might be part of the group commonly referred to as "the backpackers". These people often put themselves on a tighter budget than other travelers, or they love exploring on their own. Of course, it could also be a mix of both.

As mentioned earlier, China is not solo travel-friendly. Throughout my travels, I've run into countless frustrations that don't seem to happen elsewhere in the world. This has been everything from police checkpoints to tourist scams and language barriers to public transportation nightmares.

I remember taking a public sleeper bus with my wife to the ancient city of Pingyao. We left our hotel earlier in the day and were scheduled to arrive sometime late that night. We were awakened at 2am by the bus attendant who motioned us to get off the bus. In a daze, we grabbed our belongings and stepped off the bus. Before we could get our bearings, the bus drove off leaving us alone on the side of the highway.

" What the...?! Where are we? How are we supposed to get to our hostel in Pingyao?"

Personally, I love the stories these frustrations create. It's part of what makes the whole journey an adventure! In the end, we hitched a ride on a scooter to go into town and finally found our hostel. It was about 3:30am before we finally fell asleep.

Perhaps this story excites you, or maybe it terrifies you. Not everybody has the same enthusiasm for solo travel, and that's okay. The benefits of solo travel are the opportunity to walk that extra mile away from the tourist crowds to see a more authentic side of China. It's the ability to order food from a small hole-in-the-wall or play a game of Chinese chess with old men in the street.

Even if you're part of a tour group, see if there are free times or other opportunities to explore beyond the bubble they've created for you. More often than not, you'll be rewarded for your effort.

Step 1

GETTING A VISA TO CHINA

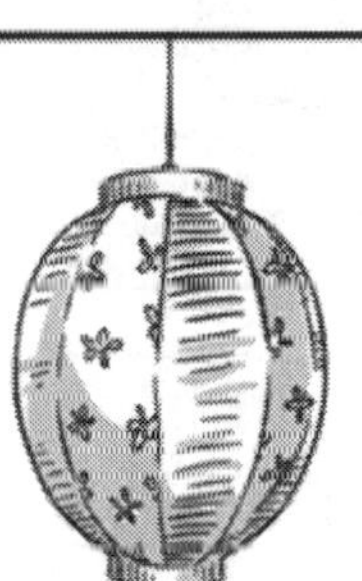

Applying for a Chinese Visa

One of the first things you need to think about when planning your trip to China is the visa. With very few exceptions, the majority of travelers will need to have obtained a Chinese visa prior to arrival in the country. Overall, the process is streamlined, but you will still need to plan for enough time to get the appropriate documents together and apply for the visa.

It is best to apply for a visa at least one month prior to your departure date. In the rare case that your application is denied for lack of proper documents, you'll have enough time to correct the mistake and try again.

The processing of your visa application typically takes 4-7 business days, and the consular costs vary by country. It is possible to expedite the process, but as you might guess, the fees jump significantly.

When applying for a tourist visa, you'll need to make sure you have the following:

1. A passport with at least 6 months of validity based on your trip date and two empty visa pages.

2. A copy of your passport information page.
3. China visa application form.
4. Two standard passport-sized photos.
5. A letter of invitation or proof of itinerary.

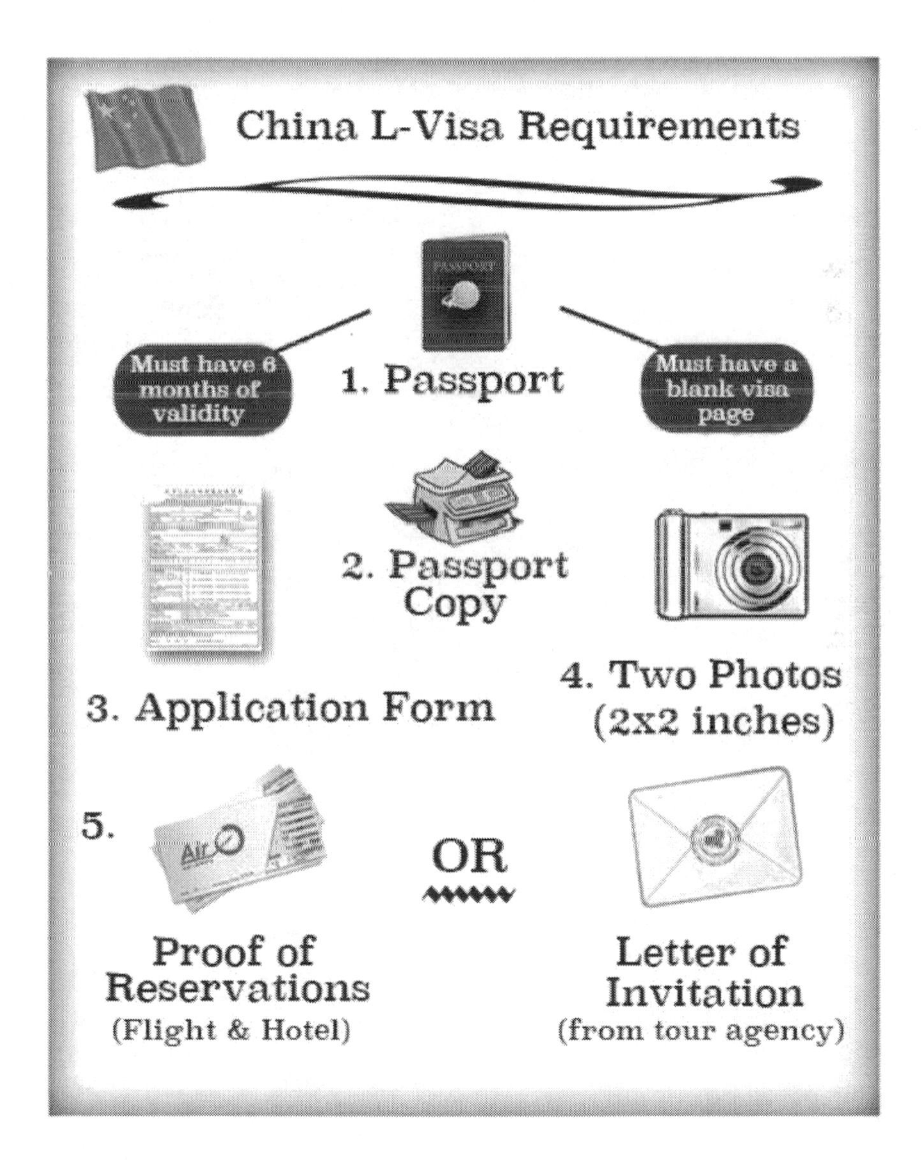

Where and how you apply for a Chinese visa varies depending on where you live. In countries such as Denmark, Canada, the United Kingdom, and many other European countries, one can apply for a visa through the *Chinese Visa Application Service Center* or "CVASC" for short.

If you live in the United States, you will need to apply at the *Chinese Consular Office*, the location of which varies based on which state you reside.

For almost every country, it's important to note that visa applications submitted by mail are no longer accepted. Applications need to be delivered directly to the CVASC or Chinese Consular Office. If you are unable to hand-deliver your application personally, you may have someone deliver it on your behalf such as a close friend, family member, or a visa agency (for a fee).

Which Visa Should You Apply For

As you fill out your China visa application form, you'll be asked to list the kind of visa you need. As a tourist, you'll want to request a standard L (Tourist) visa.

To make things slightly more complicated, though, the tourist visa has a number of different options including validity, stay limit and number of entries. There's no added cost to any of these options, so it's best to request a multi-entry visa with the longest validity, which is up to 10 years, and the longest stay limit, which is up to 60 days for tourists.

As mentioned earlier, although the vast majority of travelers will need a China tourist visa (L), there are a select few cases where you might be eligible for a newer visa offering known as the China transit visa.

China Transit Visas

Warning: The China transit visa is probably one of the most confusing and frustrating new visa options available to travelers. No other topic fills my email inbox with more questions than this!

Before I attempt to explain this option and all of its complexities, here's the bottom line: Unless you are absolutely sure that you are eligible to receive the transit visa, I would recommend opting for a traditional China visa instead.

China's transit visa (G), also known as "visa-free" or "Travel Without a Visa (TWOV)", is offered in 24-, 72- and 144-hour time periods. If you are planning a vacation that has a short layover in China or perhaps a cruise that ports in China, you may be able to enjoy a short stay without the hassle of applying for a formal visa.

China's Visa-Free Transit policy is available for individuals who hold a passport from one of 53 different countries (listed below) and allows these travelers to move about specific regions for 144 hours or less.

Which Chinese Cities Offer Transit Visas?

As of publication, there are twenty cities in China where travelers can take advantage of the transit visa policy.

These cities include Beijing, Shanghai, Guangzhou, Hangzhou, Chengdu, Wuhan, Xiamen, Qingdao, Kunming, Tianjin, Shenyang, Dalian, Nanjing, Shijiazhuang, Qinhuangdao, Changsha, Guilin, Xi'an, Harbin and Chongqing.

There are additional Chinese cities that are in the process of implementing the 72- and 144-hour transit visa, so do your research again before assuming this list is up-to-date.

Which Countries Qualify?

Not every single country passport is eligible for China's transit visa. Thankfully, there's a good chance that yours is. Check below to make sure that your home country is on the list:

- **European countries**: United Kingdom, Russia, Cyprus, Ireland, Romania, Bulgaria, Serbia, Ukraine, Bosnia-Herzegovina, Croatia, Macedonia, Montenegro, and Albania, Belarus, Monaco.
- **American countries**: United States, Brazil, Canada, Argentina, Chile, and Mexico.
- **Asian countries**: Japan, Korea, Brunei, Singapore, Qatar, and United Arab Emirates.

- **Schengen Agreement countries**: Belgium, Austria, Denmark, Czech Republic, Finland, Estonia, Germany, France, Iceland, Greece, Hungary, Lithuania, Italy, Latvia, Malta, Luxemburg, Portugal, Netherlands, Poland, Slovenia, Sweden, Spain, Slovakia, and Switzerland.
- **Oceania countries**: New Zealand and Australia.

If your country is not listed above, you should contact your local Chinese embassy to find out what provisions they have for you with regards to the China transit visa.

What Documents are Required for China's Transit Visa?

Although there is no application that you need to fill out and submit prior to landing in one of China's transit visa ports, you will need to have the following with you:

- **A valid passport**: Obviously! You'll have that with you anyway to board your flight.
- **An Arrival/Departure Card** that is complete including nationality, name, flight number, passport number, place of issuance, visa number, date of birth, gender, and purpose of visit. You can get this at the airport counter.
- **A visa for a third region or country** if required. If your country of destination doesn't require a visa, you can ignore this.

- **A ticket with a confirmed seat number** for the next flight that leaves within 24, 72 or 144 hours (see "Prerequisites" below for more details). This is important. They want to know that you are already booked to leave within the required time period.

Prerequisites for Transit Visa Application

There are a few very important things to note before attempting to take advantage of China's transit visa.

- The 72 or 144 hours doesn't actually start until 12:00am the day after arriving in a city that holds the policy. For example, if a person arrived in Shanghai on October 4th at 9:00pm, with a 144-hour transit visa they would be required to leave by 11:59pm on October 10th.
- When passengers are traveling to or from one of the twenty cities with the visa-free transit policy, they are unable to stop in any other Chinese city. The only cities that are an exception to this rule are Hong Kong, Taiwan, and Macau as they are considered third regions. For example, if your next flight went from Shanghai to Beijing, you would not be able to take advantage of the 144-hour visa while passengers traveling from Shanghai to Macau would be able to stay in Shanghai with the 144-hour visa.
- It is required that passengers leave from the same airport at which they arrived. The only known exception to this

rule is Shanghai, which allows you to leave from either Pudong Airport or Hongqiao.

***VERY IMPORTANT*:** A 2015 incident involving two travelers from New Zealand highlights the need to make sure that you're not stopping in any other Chinese cities when trying to take advantage of China's transit visas.

Two ladies were traveling from Turkey to Beijing on their way back to New Zealand, planning to take advantage of Beijing's 72-hour visa policy (at the time, the policy allowed for 72 hours, not 144 hours). They didn't realize that their flight stopped in Urumqi on the way to Beijing, the capital of China's Xinjiang region. Travelers disembarked the plane and had to go through Urumqi customs before continuing to Beijing.

These two travelers, who didn't have a Chinese visa in their passport, were held at the Urumqi airport and later a detention center since they didn't have the right paperwork. I've only heard of this happening once, but it does drive home the point that you need to *check your plans carefully* instead of just assuming that you can take advantage of the transit visa.

In the end, these two travelers were released, but not without a lot of headache, intervention from their embassy, and time wasted.

What is the Procedure to Get the Visa?

Once you arrive at one of the twenty cities mentioned above, the process of obtaining your transit visa is quite simple. Here's a quick rundown of what you should expect:

- When checking in at your departure airport, let the airline know you wish to take advantage of the transit visa. The airline will then pass on your request to customs before you land. If you will be transitioning at the Beijing Capital International Airport, you can apply for the transit permit after arriving.
- An Arrival/Departure Card must be filled out on your flight. Flight attendants will usually pass these out within an hour before landing.
- After landing, get your luggage and visit customs. There are special lanes specifically for transit permits that should be clearly marked in the customs area. At this time, an immigrations officer should approve your request for a transit free permit. They will stamp your passport and write down the approved length of time you can stay.
- Passengers are required to register with the local police station within 24 hours of arriving if they wish to stay longer than 24 hours. If you are staying with friends or family, they must accompany you to the police station and check-in in person. If you are staying in a China hotel or hostel, they will register for you.

- You must stay in your transit city for the duration of your visit unless you are in Hangzhou or Guangzhou. If you obtain your transit permit in Hangzhou or Guangzhou, you can travel throughout the province.
- If you are unable to leave within 144 hours due to flight cancellations or medical emergencies, you will have to visit the Municipal Public Security Bureau and apply for a visa.

As you can see, there are a host of confusing rules that govern the transit visa, making it an unattractive option at the moment. It's a promising program, however, that will hopefully iron out the wrinkles over time.

Beyond the Visa: Proper Registration

I'm going to assume for the moment that you have successfully received your China visa...congratulations! The feeling of seeing your first Chinese visa glued to a page in your passport is quite elating. You have been granted permission to enter one of the most fascinating countries in the world, and you're one step closer to getting there.

Unfortunately, the visa is just that: one step. Once you arrive in China, there are still additional steps that need to be taken to make sure that you remain a legal visitor of China, even if only for a short trip. According to Chinese law, foreigners must register their presence in each place they stay the night.

For travelers, it might look like this:

- **Staying at a Hotel**: Fortunately, this is the easiest form of registration since the hotel does it for you. Once you arrive, they will take a photo copy of each traveler's passport and visa page to be sent to the local police for registration.
- **Staying at a Local Home**: Technically, if you're traveling on a foreign passport, you should register with the local

authorities when you arrive at the home of a friend, family, or home rental location. Ask where the local police station is and arrive with copies of both your passport/visa and your physical passport. In most of eastern China, this likely won't be enforced but if you're traveling around more sensitive areas of China such as Tibet or Xinjiang, it will be strictly enforced. And yes, there's always a chance the local police will not grant you permission to stay at the home.

- **Camping / Outdoor**: Again, according to Chinese law a foreigner needs to register their presence, even if you're camping in the middle of nowhere or on an old section of the Great Wall. One way to get around this is to have a local travel agency register as your "sponsor". However, most people tend to camp away from watchful eyes and are generally left alone. In most cases, the worst that can happen is that local police will come and ask you to pack up and leave.

China Visa FAQ

There are a number of questions that seem to surface whenever somebody is applying for a China visa. It's a confusing process, so don't let it discourage you!

Below are the most common questions that are asked about China visas, listed in no particular order.

Who Needs a Chinese Visa?

Chances are, if you're reading this right now, you will need to get a Chinese visa. You may not require a visa if:

- You are traveling through China on your way to your final destination and will be in the country no longer than 24 hours. In this case you must remain in your area of transit such as the airport, train station, or port.
- You are staying in one of the twenty cities that have a transit policy that allows travelers to stay for 144 hours or less on their way to their final destination. These 19 cities will allow you to spend time roaming around without a visa, but the requirements for eligibility are strict.

- You are from Brunei, Singapore, or Japan and plan to conduct business, visit family, or vacation for less than 15 days. There are stipulations here, so check with your consulate to determine what they are.
- You are traveling to Hainan through a registered travel agency and plan to stay for no more than 15 days. Your tour group should tell you whether or not you will require a visa.

How Long Can I Stay in China per Entry?

As with most Chinese visas, your stay limit can be anywhere between 30-120 days. Most of the time you can request and be granted a 60-day stay per entry (for tourists this is the maximum) but if you need something longer, you can make a special request, which can often be the case for business or family visit visas.

More than likely the Chinese consulate will require you to give a reason for this special request, and it's entirely up to them to determine whether or not they give you an extended stay visa.

Can I Apply for a 10-Year Visa?

Beginning in 2014, China started signing reciprocal visa agreements with countries around the world that allowed for long-term visas to be issued. By mid-2017, five countries benefited from these long-term visas. They include:

- United States: Maximum ten-year visa for tourists.
- United Kingdom: Maximum two-year visa for tourists (China does offer five- and ten-year visas for "eligible persons" but doesn't clarify who that might be).
- Canada: Maximum nine-year eleven-month visa for tourists.
- Argentina: Maximum ten-year visa for tourists.
- Brazil: Maximum five-year visa for tourists.

If you don't see your country listed above, check the Chinese embassy in your country to determine what kind of visa you are eligible for.

Can I Work on a China Tourist Visa?

Technically no, you can't. Nor should you. If you get caught working for a Chinese company while living on a tourist visa, there will certainly be punishment both for you and the company that has hired you.

Any legitimate business or school should provide you with a work visa. If they ask you to make "visa runs" on your ten-year visa, get the heck out of that situation as quickly as you can! As recently as 2018, China has thrown foreigners in jail for working with illegitimate businesses.

Do I Need an Invitation Letter or Confirmed Flight Tickets?

As a tourist, China usually requires either a letter of invitation (usually from a travel agency) or confirmed round-trip flight tickets and hotel reservations in order to apply for a visa.

For some people, this may present a problem. For example, what if you're taking a train in from Kazakhstan or you're crossing the border from Hong Kong into China? In these cases, unless you're using a travel agency, you won't have flights to prove your entrance or exit.

As crazy as it may sound, this annoying policy requires that you purchase refundable flight tickets (and sometimes hotel reservations) to present with your visa application. You need to make certain that the tickets you are purchasing are fully refundable. They're often the more expensive tickets to purchase, and I recommend doing so directly from an airline instead of through an Online Travel Agency (OTA) like Expedia or Kayak.

Once your Chinese visa is issued, you can cancel your tickets and reservations to get a refund. Don't worry, this will not present any future problems for you. China's visas are not tied to specific flights or hotels, and as long as you enter through an open international port, the visa alone will be sufficient.

What Are the Other Types of Visas?

There are a number of visas one can apply for, and I admit it can be confusing. Which one you choose depends on your reasons for traveling. Listed here are a few of the most common types of visas with a brief explanation:

- **Tourist Visa (L):** This is the most common visa and probably the one you'll be applying for if you are planning to vacation or visiting family in China. This is the only visa that an individual can apply for without help from a business, school, or government agency.
- **Business Visa (F and M):** While the M visa is the more typical business visa, the F visa is for individuals invited to China for investigations, non-commercial exchanges, education, science related ventures, and health reasons. These visas require an invitation letter from an existing China business.
- **Student Visa (X):** This visa allows foreign students to study or perform fieldwork in China for either less than 6 months (X2) or longer than 6 months (X1). There are special forms that must be filled out by the educational institution for this visa.
- **Work Visa (Z):** If you want to work in China and get paid, you will need a Work Visa. Your employer is responsible for sending you the proper documents such as a Visa Notification Letter and Employee Permit.

- **Family Reunion Visas (S and Q):** This is relatively new and allows family members to visit loved ones who are working or going to school in China. Family members that are able to use this visa include siblings, spouses, in-laws, children, parents, and grandparents.

How Do I Extend a Visa?

If you wish to change visas in China (for example, from a tourist visa to a work/student visa) you can usually do so without leaving the country, but it will need to be done well before the expiration of your current visa. You will need to apply for this at the *Public Security Bureau Entry and Exit Administration Office* or "PSB" for short.

Public Security Bureau = 公安局 Gōng'ān jú

When applying to extend your current visa – for example if you want to add another 30 days to your tourist visa – you will also need to visit the Public Security Bureau. Tourist visas cannot be extended more than 30 days without leaving the country, and in most cases the effort isn't worth the extra time.

Step 2:

PREPARING TO TRAVEL TO CHINA

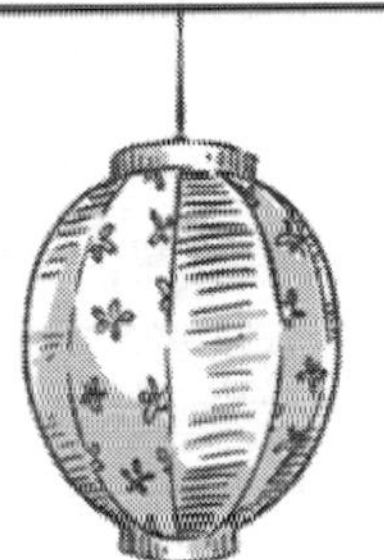

Preparing for China

Now that a visa has been glued to a blank page of your passport, this whole China thing starts to get real!

In addition to planning out an itinerary for your travels and figuring out where you're going to stay, you also need to set aside time to work out everything that needs to be prepared *before* you get on your China-bound plane. This includes arranging the documents you'll need, getting any vaccinations, determining how you want to deal with money in China, ironing out your itinerary, etc.

Whatever you do, don't leave these important tasks to the last minute. There's nothing worse than running around on the week before your departure date, trying to arrange things with your bank, getting shots, and organizing your documents.

What Documents Do I Need?

Aside from carrying your physical passport with your China visa, there are a few things to consider with documentation. Some of this should go without saying, but I find that it's good to have a checklist *just to be sure* I haven't forgotten anything.

Document Checklist for Travelers:

✓ **Your passport with visa**: This is necessary for any international travel. Double check that your passport is valid for at least six months from the date of your planned departure, otherwise you'll need to consider renewing your passport before you go.

✓ **A copy of your passport & visa page**: I always advise travelers to keep these copies in a separate bag from your original documents, just in case you lose your bag.

✓ **Your health insurance card**: Whether it's a card or just a printout, you need your travel insurance ID and phone numbers that you would call in case there's a medical emergency. Learn more in the chapter about healthcare in China.

- ✓ **A printout of your flight details**: You want this printout to include your ticket number and the phone number of your travel agent or airline in case you need to contact them.

That's really it. What you *don't* need are things like a social security card or even your driver's license. China does not recognize the International Driver's Permit (IDP), so bringing your driver's license along won't do you much good. Also, as we'll cover in the next chapter, you won't need to bring proof of vaccination or immunization.

What Vaccines Do I Need?

Before I dive into vaccinations, I strongly suggest that you consult your doctor at least six weeks prior to your trip to get professional medical advice. What I'm about to share with you is based upon recommendations from the US Centers for Disease Control and Prevention but should only be used in consultation with a licensed medical doctor in your own country.

For an up-to-date list of the recommended vaccines, visit the CDC website here:

www.travelchinacheaper.com/cdc

For visitors and tourist, China does not *require* any particular vaccines unless you are arriving from a country that has a high risk of yellow fever. If you're traveling through or are a citizen of one of these countries, which are all located in Africa, Central and South America, you'll likely already have a Yellow Fever vaccination anyway. At no point during the China visa process will you be asked for proof of immunization. The vaccines you choose are entirely voluntary and although many of us were immunized as children, the schedules have changed over time, so it's worth comparing what you have versus what is now recommended.

It also makes a difference where you are traveling in China and how long you will be there. If you never plan to leave the major cities such as Beijing, Shanghai, or Hong Kong, routine immunizations usually cover you well. These routine immunizations include:

- MMR: Measles-mumps-rubella
- Tdap: The tetanus vaccine
- Varicella: The chickenpox vaccine
- Polio vaccine
- Your Annual Flu Shot

For those travelers who have plans to travel outside the major cities but won't be in the country for very long, the CDC recommends that you add:

- Hepatitis A: There are parts of China where contaminated food or water puts you at risk for Hep A.
- Typhoid: This is recommended for those who are staying in the homes of friends or relatives in smaller cities.

Finally, if you plan to venture into rural areas of China or hope to stay for a month or longer, the CDC recommends you discuss the following immunizations with your doctor:

- Hepatitis B: Since this is usually spread by blood or contaminated needles, you'll want to make sure you have this vaccination if you have any plans of getting a tattoo, piercing or any type of medical procedure in China.
- Japanese Encephalitis: This is particularly important in rural areas if you plan to spend a lot of time outdoors.
- Polio: The CDC recommends this vaccine for those visiting the Xinjiang region, working at a healthcare facility or doing humanitarian aid of any kind.
- Rabies: This is recommended if there's any particular reason you'll be around animals while in China.
- Yellow Fever: There is no risk of yellow fever in China, but you'll need this vaccine if you're coming from a country that does have a risk of yellow fever. You can find this list on the CDC website:

  www.travelchinacheaper.com/yellow-fever-countries

- Malaria: If you plan to do outdoor hiking or camping in places that might have mosquitos in China, taking measures to prevent malaria is a good idea.

Now if you're like me, you look at this list and your head starts spinning. Don't worry! Most of us have all the required immunizations we need for short-term travel around China, but there might be one or two you want to add for the sake of precaution, particularly if you'll be visiting rural areas or doing a lot of outdoor activities.

The bottom line is that you need to ask your personal physician what they think. Schedule an appointment at least six weeks in advance of your trip so that you have plenty of time to add any immunizations you don't have.

All About the Money

It's important to understand how to get and use money in China before you go. It would be quite a challenge to be stuck in China without access to your money!

For this reason, in this chapter we're going to talk about how to get or exchange money in China, discuss the best way to pay for things, and include a checklist of things to do before you leave.

China operates with a system of currency known as the Renminbi, which roughly translates as "The People's Currency". You'll often hear this money referred to as "yuan" or "kuai", which are both terms in the Chinese language that refer to a unit of renminbi.

China does use coins in their currency; however, the majority of money takes the form of printed banknotes, the most common of which are ¥1, ¥5, ¥10, ¥20, ¥50 and ¥100.

No matter what kind of currency you use, whether U.S. dollars, Euros, pounds or any other global currency, you're going to need to find a way to convert that to Renminbi in order to make almost any purchase in China.

How to Get or Exchange Money in China

When I first started traveling around China, I remember walking around China with wads of cash or standing in line at the bank to convert it into Traveler's Checks or US dollars. As a teacher, I was paid in cash, and I didn't have a bank account. It didn't seem necessary because there were very few shops around town that accepted bank cards!

Fast forward about 12 years. I now rarely use cash, and I haven't stepped foot in a Chinese bank in a year. I pay for almost everything - from groceries in a store to a bottle of water from a street vendor - using my phone or Chinese debit card. While travelers may not have the same luxury of time to set up these convenient forms of payment like long-term expatriates do, you're going to run into it everywhere you go.

Despite incredible advances in mobile payment options in China, the truth is that unless you plan to travel around China for longer than a month, your best payment option for most things is going to be cash. For this reason, it's important to understand the best ways to exchange your home currency for RMB. These options include:

- **Bringing Cash**: By law, travelers are allowed to take the equivalent of approximately US$5,000 in foreign currency into or out of China without declaring it at customs. While I don't suggest you ever travel with that much money on you, it's not a bad idea to keep an emergency fund of your home currency with you. Currency can be converted at the airport or at most hotels, although the best rates are found at a local bank. Beware that lines are long at Chinese banks, and the process isn't always fast, so when it comes to getting money into China, I don't recommend this method for anything other than emergency funds.
- **Using Chinese ATMs**: No matter where you are in China, you're usually only a hundred meters or less away from an ATM. Thankfully, you'll find that most ATMs in China accept Visa, MasterCard, Cirrus, and JCB, so it's not difficult to pull out cash from your home bank account once you arrive here. The benefit to this method

is that it's convenient, and you're not always carrying around wads of cash everywhere you go. The disadvantage is that you won't get the most favorable exchange rate, and you're stuck if your bank freezes your card on fears that its use in a foreign country constitutes fraud. This happens quite often, which is why I always recommend you call to put an international travel alert on your bank account.

- **Buying Traveler's Checks**: Traveler's Checks used to be a common way to secure money while abroad. Since nobody can cash those checks but you, you eliminate the fear of losing them or having them stolen. The problem here is twofold: first, there are few banks that still issue traveler's checks. Second, it's a hassle to visit a Chinese bank in order to cash these checks. At the very least, you'll need to budget two to three hours, if not more, to spend at a Chinese bank converting the check to renminbi.

What's This WeChat and Alipay?

As I said earlier, payment methods have changed quite a bit in China, and this is a good thing. In many ways, China has been able to surpass Western countries in the widespread adoption of alternate methods of payment.

If you've never heard of WeChat or Alipay, you can think of these phone apps as Chinese social media platforms that facilitate payment similar to Apple Pay or Google Wallet. This is the most common method for local Chinese to use for payment because of how easy it is. You connect your Chinese bank to your WeChat or Alipay account and then scan a QR code to make payment.

But what about travelers who don't have a Chinese bank account? Unfortunately, China has made it extremely difficult, if not impossible for you as a short-term traveler. In January of 2018 WeChat announced that it would allow WeChat users to add a foreign credit card to their account, but I have yet to meet anybody, including myself, who has been able to make it work. Hopefully these restrictions will change in the future, but for now WeChat and Alipay aren't a reliable method of payment for short-term travelers. You'll have to stick with cash and cards.

Money · A China Traveler's Checklist

Now that you understand how to get cash and how to pay for things in China, I want to quickly run through a checklist of things you should do prior to your departure:

- ✓ **Contact Your Bank**: Let them know that you'll be traveling abroad to China and using your card. They'll usually add a note on the account to make sure it doesn't get frozen while you're gone.
- ✓ **Double Check Your PIN Number**: If you're like me, you don't pull cash out of an ATM very often back home, so it's understandable if you've forgotten your PIN number. Double check the PIN number for your debit or credit

card, so you can pull cash without problems in China. Sometimes I even tell people to test their PIN at one of their bank ATMs just to be sure everything works.

- ✓ **Bring Cash**: I always tell my friends and family to pull out at least a US$200-$300 worth of cash before their journey. I keep this money as an "emergency fund" just in case the bank decides to freeze my account, or I somehow lose my wallet.
- ✓ **Establish a Backup Plan**: Imagine just for a moment that the worst does happen: your wallet with all of your credit cards is stolen, you have a week or more left in China, and you don't have enough cash to cover you. What do you do? In a dire situation, you can reach out to your embassy for help, but this should be a last resort. I recommend keeping an extra credit card in your suitcase, preferably from a different bank. There are other ways to protect yourself; the key is to establish a good backup plan.

Planning Your Itinerary

One of the most common questions I receive from travelers has to do with their itinerary. Just the other day I had a traveler literally copy-and-paste their entire three-week itinerary and ask me *"What do you think?"*

The truth is that travel is such a personal experience. We all travel for different reasons and with different expectations, which means that there is no "one size fits all" itinerary. If that's what you're hoping for, I'm afraid you'll be disappointed. That said, a simple search on Google will provide you with plenty of example itineraries to choose from. As you start borrowing these ideas for your own itinerary creation, ask yourself a few questions.

First, *"Is my schedule flexible or rigid?"* Truth be told, travelers with rigid schedules usually find themselves frustrated in China. Flight delays, traffic jams, unexpected changes, etc. will happen in China. It all points to the fact that the more flexibility you can work into your itinerary, the better.

Second, ask yourself: *"Can this realistically be accomplished in a day?"* I know some people who arrive in Beijing thinking they can hit all the major sites in two or three days. This is a pipe dream. Chinese cities are larger than you realize and take much longer to traverse than you'd imagine. You might be able to do the Summer Palace in the morning and stop by the Temple of Heaven in the afternoon, but that's really it. When you're done, it's likely you'll be so tired of subways and walking that you'll be begging to go back to the hotel.

Finally, and probably before anything else, I would ask yourself: *"What do I really want to get from this trip to China?"* There are so many amazing places to see in China, and it's tempting to think you can - or should - see all of it. Instead, try to vet what you place on your itinerary through the lens of your ultimate goal. Are you a history buff? Do you prefer architecture? Are you interested in good shopping opportunities? The answer to these questions should dictate your itinerary more than what some travel agencies put in their "package tour".

Recommended China Travel Guide Books

While I'm doing my best in this guide to cover everything you need to know *before* you travel to China, there are plenty of great books that do a great job telling you what to do *once you arrive* in China. I've worked as a writer and editor for *Lonely Planet, DK, Fodor's,* and even my own Xinjiang guide, and I can tell you the end product represents hundreds of hours of hard work and research. These travel guidebooks are comprehensive, sometimes overwhelming, and they're meant to help you plan your itinerary.

Fair warning: most of these are heavy, hefty books that take up a lot of room in your suitcase. Even if you like using a physical book to plan your travel, I suggest you purchase the digital version to take with you on the road instead. Here are the guide books I usually recommend to travelers based on the type of travel you plan to do in China.

- **Lonely Planet China**: Lonely Planet China is the gold standard of travel guides for China. It's geared toward the independent traveler who wants to avoid travel agencies and do everything on their own. You won't find a ton of colorful maps or in-depth history within the Lonely Planet, but you will get an overview of everything there is to see, how to get there, and how much it all costs.
- **DK Eyewitness Travel Guide China**: Whereas the Lonely Planet is very text heavy, the DK travel guide is very colorful with lots of diagrams and maps. If you're planning to stay in the major travel areas (i.e. Beijing, Xi'an, Chengdu, Shanghai, etc.), you'll find this book particularly helpful.
- **Fodor's China**: Fodor's markets this guide by claiming that it's like "having a friend in China". I'd agree; it's a healthy balance between the necessary details that Lonely Planet does so well and the illustrations that make DK such a useful guide. The difference is that Fodor's does a better job covering all of China than DK and offers better illustrations than Lonely Planet.
- **The Rough Guides China**: At the risk of giving you too many options, I'd like to offer the Rough Guide for

anybody that is a true backpacker. If your goal is to travel on the leanest budget and plan everything you need to know, Rough Guide is an amazing resource.

Packing for China

I don't know about you, but sometimes packing for a trip can be one of the most stressful parts of traveling.

It has nothing to do with the choice of suitcase versus backpack or packing light versus packing for any situation. No, most of it has to do with not knowing what is provided in a hotel room or what is available for purchase at a store. Does my wife need to bring her hair dryer? Do I need to pack a plug converter for all my electronics? Can I buy batteries once I get there, or do I need to bring extras from home?

In this chapter, I'd like to run through what you can expect to find in a hotel room as well as the availability of common items that foreign travelers often ask about. This should give you some helpful direction while packing, but if you want even more help, you can find a full packing checklist in the appendix portion of this guide.

What You'll Find in a Chinese Hotel Room

The good news is that on average, Chinese hotels offer more free amenities than their Western counterparts. It's not uncommon for a Chinese hotel to provide guests with a new toothbrush, toothpaste, shampoo, soap, comb, hair dryer and hair cap. For many people, traveling around China with nothing more than some deodorant and makeup works just fine.

Of course, don't be surprised if you don't like the flavor of toothpaste. One of the most popular flavors I've noticed at Chinese hotels is green tea toothpaste. Needless to say, it's not my favorite.

Every hotel I've stayed in China has provided a hair dryer in the bathroom. The quality of the appliance may not be great, but at least it's there. If you want to bring your own hair dryer, hair straightener, or other bathroom appliance, double check to make sure that it is rated for 220 volts. For example, many hair dryers in the United States are only manufactured to accept 110 volts and plugging it into China's standard 220-volt outlets can be disastrous and quite dangerous.

Availability of Common Items for Travelers

As you pack your suitcase in preparation for your China journey, there are a number of things to consider. China is quickly becoming a developed country where you can find almost anything you're looking for, but it may not be easy to do so.

For this reason, I'd like to list for you some of the most common items travelers ask me about and list them as either "Easy to purchase in China" or "Difficult to purchase in China".

Easy to Purchase in China: The following items are readily available in stores throughout China, in both large and small cities alike.

- **Most toiletries:** If you lose your toothbrush or run out of makeup, it's usually quite easy to find these things at a Chinese store. The only exception would be deodorant, which is less common in China, particularly outside the major cities.
- **OTC Medicines:** Pharmacies can be found on every street corner in China and they sell quite a few over the counter (OTC) drugs. They'll all be listed in Chinese characters, though, so you'll need to translate what you need before you arrive.
- **Batteries:** Whether you need AA, AAA, D, watch batteries or even camera batteries, they're usually not difficult to find.
- **Camera Accessories:** If you need an extra SD card for your camera or a new battery, these accessories are readily sold at camera stores in every Chinese city.

Difficult to Purchase in China: The following items are harder to find as you travel around China, and it's best to make sure you pack them in your luggage before you leave.

- **Deodorant:** Deodorant is not commonly used in China (a fact which you'll quickly discover if you travel on a crowded city bus!); therefore, the choices - if there are any - are quite scarce.

- **Pepto Bismol:** Chances are, at some point during your travels your stomach will not appreciate the new cuisine you're feeding it. Having some Pepto Bismol handy can be a lifesaver.
- **Hand Sanitizer:** Not all bathrooms in China offer soap, so you'll want to bring your own hand sanitizer since it's not commonly sold in China stores.
- **Sunscreen:** If you need sunscreen, it's best to bring your own. There's plenty of sunscreen available in China, but since the Asian culture values white skin over tan skin, all of the sunscreen available in China also come with a skin-whitening ingredient.
- **Gluten-Free Foods:** If you have certain dietary restrictions such as gluten intolerance or lactose intolerance, I'm pretty sure I don't have to tell you that you have quite the challenge ahead of you in China.

China Traveler Packing List

Now that you understand what is and isn't readily available in China, the next step is to pack your own suitcase. What you pack depends on a number of factors including the weather for where you'll be traveling in China, the time of year you are traveling, and your own preferences.

Still, if you would like a general packing list to make sure you're not forgetting anything, I've included an example travel packing list to use in the appendix of this book.

Purchasing Your China Flights

Like it or not, transportation often eats up the largest chunk of your travel budget. This is especially true in China, where expensive international flights are sometimes unavoidable. Because of this, I'd like to spend some time outlining what I've learned about purchasing tickets to and from China.

How to Purchase Good International Flights

There are flights to China...and then there are *good flights* to China. Unless you've made the trip multiple times, it's hard to know what to look for. I realize that you might be restrained by budget, timeframe, or even final destination, but here are some thoughts on getting a good flight to China.

- **Avoid the Temptation to Buy the Cheapest Ticket**: When you search for international flights to China, you'll likely run into a few fares that are considerably cheaper than all the others. I'm talking hundreds of dollars cheaper - and I know how tempting that might be. Don't do it! In my experience, these flights represent the oldest, most uncomfortable planes. They don't have personal movie entertainment, the food is horrible, and the leg room is non-existent. Unless you're on a tight budget, your sanity is worth a couple hundred extra dollars. I know mine is.

- **Arrive at a Decent Hour**: I recommend you avoid flights that arrive any time after 10pm, particularly if this is your first time in China. Public transportation has usually stopped for the night by the time you get out of customs, and it's more difficult to find help in the middle of the night. In my experience, the only time I've been ripped off by taxis is between the hours of 11pm and 6am.
- **Choose Your Airport Wisely**: China's major cities are so large that many of them have multiple airports. Some are convenient while others aren't. For example, Shanghai has two airports: one on the west side of town and one on the east side of town. Hongqiao, on the west side, has a convenient subway stop and train station, but it doesn't handle as many international flights. Pudong, on the other hand, is far to the east and is where many international flights land. While traveling around China, if you take a train or flight into Hongqiao as you prepare to depart internationally, transiting to the Pudong airport is a huge hassle. I've done it once, and it took me almost four hours. The bottom line: check your airport codes carefully.

Tips for Saving Money on International Flights

I know I just told you to avoid the cheapest international fares to China if you can, but there are other ways that you can save money on your flight purchase. All it takes is a little forethought and a bit of preparation, and you could save literally hundreds of dollars on your international flights. Here are some great tips for you:

- **Sell Your Extra Checked Baggage**: If you're traveling as a tourist with two checked bags, you need to reconsider your packing! Most international flights offer two free checked bags, but if you're not using both of them, you can sell that unused space. It's called being an "air courier" and it was surprisingly easy in my experience. I listed my flight and was sent a manifest of the goods that I would be checking in. The luggage was delivered to me at the US airport and picked up outside baggage claim in China. I was paid over $150 per piece of luggage! When I first heard about it, it sounded sketchy. After trying it, I was blown away. I created a video about the process that you can watch here:

  www.travelchinacheaper.com/air-courier-video

- **Don't Fly on Chinese Holidays**: When planning your trip to China, it's critical to be aware of national holidays that may affect pricing of international flights (not to mention any domestic tickets). The Chinese New Year is the obvious one, but there are other smaller holidays that you might want to consider scheduling around. For a list of this year's holidays, some of which are floating holidays, check this link:

  www.travelchinacheaper.com/chinese-holidays

- **Check Domestic OTAs**: There are plenty of OTAs, or "Online Travel Agencies" to choose from: Kayak, Orbitz,

Expedia, etc. Perhaps you have your favorite, and I don't want to discourage you from researching flights there. While researching flights, I recommend you also check China's domestic OTAs such as eLong or Trip (owned by Ctrip). They almost always have better pricing on domestic flights, but sometimes you can find great deals on international flights there too.

- **Don't Forget to Earn Miles!** Because international flight tickets are usually a larger purchase, I often recommend US travelers to look into travel credit cards that can help them earn miles/points. In many cases, these credit cards require spending a specific amount of money in a two- to three-month time period but reward you with hundreds of dollars' worth of miles/points. For example, if you're going to fly Delta to China, by applying for the American Express Delta card and purchasing the Delta flight with the new card, you can earn double miles on the flight purchase, miles for actually flying, and then up to 60,000 bonus miles for reaching the spending limit within three months. That ends up being the equivalent of two or three free domestic flights! I don't recommend credit cards for those who can't pay off the balance, but if you're going to purchase these flight tickets anyway, you might as well get all the benefits you can from it!

Step 3:

FINDING ACCOMMODATION IN CHINA

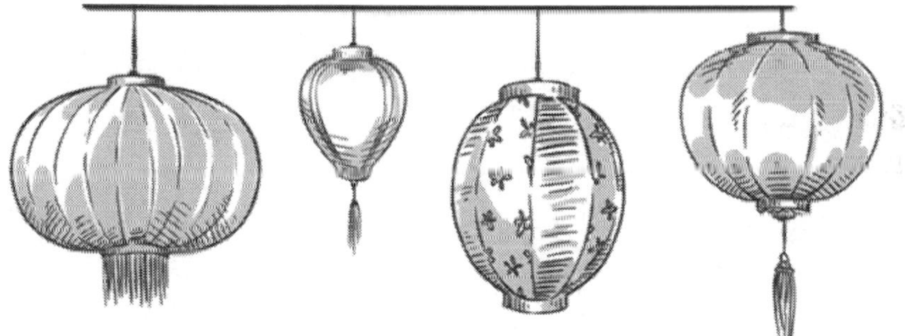

What to Expect with Chinese Hotels

It doesn't matter if you're planning to stay in five-star hotels or share a bunk bed in a youth hostel, everybody needs to sleep somewhere. Thankfully, China has a diverse selection of hotels from which to choose that will please almost any budget.

Before we dive into what you should expect when it comes to this selection of Chinese hotels, however, there are two important facts you should understand:

1. Foreign travelers in China must be registered in every place they stay. This means that when you check into a hotel, they will ask for your passport so that they can make a copy and register you with the police.
2. Not every Chinese hotel is allowed to accept foreigners. Although there are dirt-cheap hotels all across the country, China considers it a "loss of face" (an embarrassment) to allow a foreigner to stay in one of these cheaper varieties. To make sure that a foreign traveler is staying in an acceptable establishment, hotels must apply for the right to accept foreign travelers and this application is only approved if the hotel is rated as three stars or higher.

If you're the type of traveler who books their hotels online ahead of your trip, you shouldn't have any problems. Almost every hotel you find listed in English-language online booking websites is registered to accept foreign travelers.

If, however, you're the type of traveler who likes to go with the flow and find a hotel when you arrive, you might run into cases where a hotel won't sell you a room. There's nothing you can do except ask around for another hotel that permits foreign travelers. It will probably be more expensive, but each small town in China has at least one.

What to Expect · Chinese Hotels

When you look at pictures of Chinese hotels online, they look to be very similar to what you'd expect in the West. In some ways, they are the same. In many ways, they aren't. Major international brands like Hilton and Radisson will feel familiar, but in general you should expect hotels to have their own "Chinese characteristics". Let's run down a list of ways in which Chinese hotels might be a bit different than your expectations:

- **Chinese Hotel Beds:** The Chinese culture tends to think that soft beds are unhealthy for the body, so you're likely to be surprised by the firmness of a hotel bed. That's normal. Also, a standard room in China consists of two, separate twin beds. If you'd like to sleep with your significant other, you'll want to specifically request a queen or king bedroom.

- **Room Amenities:** Chinese hotels are usually stocked with the normal amenities: a nice flat-screen TV, some coffee and tea, and a mini bar. The difference you need to be aware of is that it's almost impossible to find a good English TV channel, and you'll never run across decaf coffee. One thing you will find familiar is that they still grossly overprice their mini-bar items just like everywhere else in the world.
- **Smoking:** Smoking is a common habit in China, and although there are rules against smoking in hotel rooms, those rules are often ignored without consequence. I've been in a few Chinese hotel rooms that reek of smoke. If this happens to you, just turn around, return to the front desk, and don't be afraid to ask for another room.
- **Continental Breakfast:** If your hotel room includes breakfast, you might want to clarify whether they mean a Chinese or international breakfast. To most foreign travelers, the Chinese breakfast is interesting, to say the least. Amid the array of spicy dishes and cooked vegetables that don't seem like traditional breakfast foods, most foreign travelers end up eating only steamed bread and boiled eggs.
- **The Swimming Pool:** Swimming pools aren't a common amenity for Chinese hotels. They do exist, but it's probably not what you expect. In some cases, hotels charge extra to use the pool and offer it only as part of their spa package. Also, when you do swim, it's mandatory in China to wear a swim cap.

The good news is that you can expect to find air conditioning and heating throughout all hotels in China. Likewise, almost every hotel I've been in has plumbing that allows for toilet paper to be flushed.

Special Note: Up until the past few years, Chinese hotels have had a bad reputation for one thing: *prostitutes*. I've had these ladies knock on the door, slip cards under my door or even call the room to offer up "massage" services. Thankfully, China has cracked down on this practice recently. It still happens, though, particularly in budget hotels. My advice to travelers is to unplug the phone in your room to avoid any awkward calls at 1am and to ask who it is before opening the hotel door at night.

How to Find Good Hotels in China

For first time visitors to China, the act of actually choosing a hotel can be stressful. Unless you have a travel agency making the choice for you, it feels a bit like Russian roulette: you just don't know what you're going to get!

The fear is not without reason. I've stayed in some pretty bad hotels while traveling throughout China. Well, let me rephrase that. The hotels were fine by Chinese standards; however, by international standards, they were terrible. So, what can you do to make sure that you're choosing the best hotel possible? Here are a few things to consider as you look around online for the best Chinese hotels.

Understand the China Rating System

First things first: the star rating system in China is a joke. What gets by as a five-star hotel in China would rarely rate as a four-star anywhere else in the world. Just the fact that you can stay in a Chinese five-star hotel for less than US$100 is an indication of the standard being used here.

Most Chinese hotels are rated on an official system that runs from one to five stars. This is important because, according to Chinese policy, a foreigner is only allowed to stay the night at hotels with three or more stars. Thankfully, most of the time these hotels are perfectly acceptable and budget-friendly.

The bottom line is this: as you are searching for a Chinese hotel online, understand that a three-star hotel is the lowest rating and a four-star hotel would be considered average anywhere else in the world. The five-star rating covers a wide range of experiences, including what most travelers would consider a good business hotel all the way to a legitimate, international five-star hotel. Price is often the only indication of which five-star you're dealing with.

Staying Near Public Transport is Important

As the old saying goes, "Location, location, location". This is never truer than in China, where city blocks can often take fifteen minutes to walk, and taxis can be impossible to find anytime you need one.

The problem here is that maps can be deceiving. For example, if you look at a hotel in Beijing and see that it's only two blocks from the nearest subway stop, you may be inclined to think, "You know, that's not too far. We could save $20 a night!". The reality is that those two blocks could easily require 20-30 minutes of walking each way which can really wear on you.

In bigger cities, finding a hotel located near a strategic subway stop can mean the difference between quick transportation to your next destination or an hour of extra walking. To me, that's often worth the extra $20.

Local Booking Websites = Lots of Pictures

I enjoy using services like Expedia, Orbitz and others, but when it comes to hotels in China, they lack the one thing that really matters: the listings don't have lots and lots of photos.

While photos can definitely be deceiving, the more there are, the easier it is to get a sense of whether or not a hotel bathroom will fit your needs. It's for this reason that I usually suggest that travelers do their hotel research on local websites like the Chinese Trip (Ctrip) or the Asian booking site Agoda.

Both of these online travel agencies offer their websites in English and are able to accept most major credit cards. Best of all, because they are locally-based companies, they usually provide quite a few photos for each hotel, including shots of the front (helpful for finding the hotel when you arrive), pictures of the different rooms, and pictures of the bathrooms.

- **Trip:** www.travelchinacheaper.com/try/trip-hotels
- **Agoda:** www.travelchinacheaper.com/try/agoda

Pricing is Meaningful

As I said above, pricing is often your only indication of quality. Let's take hotels in Beijing for example. In a simple search, I came across the Junyi Runhua hotel that offers rooms for US$59/night. I also found the Hilton Beijing that offers rooms starting at US$159/night. Both are rated "5-stars", but as you can imagine, they are completely different in quality.

This might be obvious when you're dealing with an international brand like Hilton, but in most cases when you're comparing two domestic hotels side-by-side, the only indication you will have of the quality will be pricing. I'm not saying that you can't find good deals, and I'm not telling you to increase your budget. I'm only suggesting that you get what you pay for.

What to Expect with Hostels in China

If you're looking to save a bit of money and meet with other travelers along the way, hostels present an excellent option for accommodation in China. They usually offer excellent locations and unique experiences.

For example, there's a hostel in Xi'an I've stayed in that is located within the city walls not far from the train station. It's quiet, it's cheap, and (best of all) it's modeled after ancient Chinese courtyard homes. Likewise, I've enjoyed a stay at a hostel in Beijing nestled within the small alleyways of the old hutong.

While not all hostels in China are registered to accept foreign travelers, most of them are. This is particularly true if they're affiliated with Hosteling International or HostelWorld.

What to Expect · Chinese Hostels

Hostels in China are similar to what you'll find pretty much anywhere in the world: they offer basic dorm rooms, a few private rooms, bathrooms, and a common area. Each hostel offers its own set of unique amenities, but I'd like to list some of the most common things you should expect with a hostel, particularly in comparison to a hotel.

1. **Most hostels offer English-speaking staff.** While only five-star hotels have English speakers on staff, almost all hostels have at least somebody who can communicate with you in English. The reason for this is that the majority of their guests are foreigners.
2. **Hostels are about meeting people.** If you're an introvert, or if you prefer privacy when you retire for the night, a hostel might not be the best place for you. Hostels are a perfect fit for the Chinese culture because of the common areas that serve to promote interaction with other travelers. This is a mirror of the ancient courtyard houses where various family units would live in different sections of a building all disposed around a central courtyard.
3. **Hostels might be nicer than you think.** There are many times that I've preferred a hostel over a nice hotel. For example, I stayed in a hostel in Suzhou that was a quaint and beautiful little place right next to the canal. The location couldn't be beat, and the atmosphere felt so authentic. I stayed in a private room with my own bathroom, just like a hotel, but I was afforded an experience no nearby hotel offered for that price.
4. **Yes, hostels have Western toilets and hot showers.** While these toilets and showers might not be as luxurious or dependable as those in a nicer hotel, I've never been to a Chinese hostel that didn't have them.

5. **Hostels cater to tourists**. This means that you'll likely find somebody who can help arrange a tour, transportation, or show you how to get somewhere on a map. A hostel is also a great place to join a group to keep your costs down.

Staying in a hostel isn't for everybody, I realize; however, it's a fun experience that is worth a try, in my opinion.

To find a good hostel, I recommend checking out HostelWorld:

www.travelchinacheaper.com/try/hostelworld

Homestays and Camping in China

For some travelers, a simple hotel or hostel isn't adventurous enough. They may want the unique experience of staying at a local Chinese home or sleeping on somebody's couch. They might want to hike along the Great Wall and set up a tent to camp for the night. Basically, they want a more intimate view of China that is difficult to find at a large hotel chain.

While this is possible, let's look at what you should – and shouldn't do – in order to get these kinds of experiences.

Using Airbnb in China

As travel around the world continues to evolve, I've begun to see many people look to home-sharing apps like Airbnb as an accommodation option in China. When looking through their app or website, you'll notice plenty of listings all throughout China for apartments you can rent.

However, I recommend you avoid services like Airbnb completely in China.

Don't get me wrong: I love using Airbnb when I travel. But things are different in China. Remember when I mentioned the government policy saying that all foreign travelers have to register their presence wherever they go? This applies even to Airbnb, except unlike hotels which do the registration process for you, with Airbnb and similar services, you're left doing this by yourself.

Registering in China involves preparing copies of all your passports, copies of your visa, and – hardest of all – finding the darn police station! The hours spent wandering the streets in search of the police station often aren't worth the Airbnb experience.

In the past, travelers have been able to get away with not registering their stay at an Airbnb. China is starting to crack down on this, however, and I've read multiple horror stories about China Airbnb stays gone wrong.

Unless you're staying with family and friends (where you'll still have to register, by the way), I usually recommend that travelers stick with hotels and hostels in China.

Tips for Homestays and Camping

If you're interested in doing a homestay or trying some camping while traveling in China, there are a few things that I recommend:

1. **Consider a Travel Agency**. Travel agencies will have much better connections to set you up with a proper

homestay than going through a service like Airbnb. They can also help you get the appropriate permissions to camp in places like the Great Wall. If you need suggestions, I have a list of reliable China travel agencies in the appendix of this book.

2. **Lay Low**. If you decide to do a homestay or camping trip on your own, the best advice I can give is to keep a low profile. The more people who see you, the higher the chance that you'll get a visit from local police asking what you're doing. For homestays, don't make a big scene by having a big party at the house. For camping, try to set up camp away from any paths or within sight of any villages.

Step 4:
TRANSPORTATION WITHIN CHINA

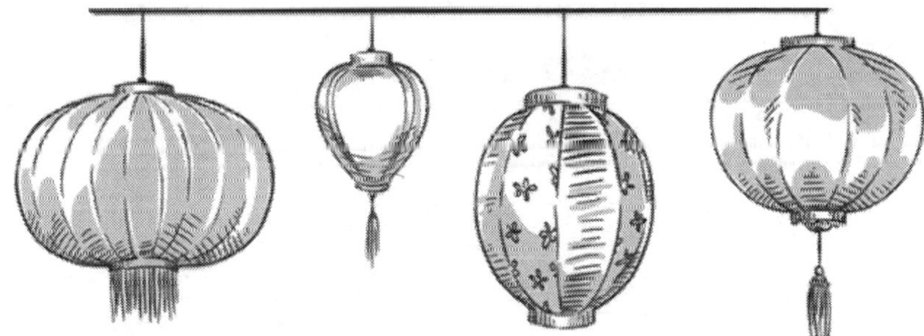

Guide to Flying in China

Chances are high that you're going to spend at least a little time in a Chinese airport during your visit to China. Whether you're flying internationally to enter and exit the country, or you're flying domestically to get from point A to point B, transiting through a local airport is a necessity.

What you'll find as you fly around China is that the experience feels very familiar. Airports are laid out the same way they are anywhere in the world: a check-in area to get your tickets and drop off baggage, a security area to invade your personal privacy, and a gate area with uncomfortable seats to wait for your flight. You still must take out your laptop when putting your bag through the scanner, and you're still allowed only one carry-on and one personal item on the airplane.

There are some important differences to consider when flying in and around China, though. For example, when checking a bag in China, the standard weight limit is 20 kilograms (44 lbs.), as opposed to the 23 kilograms (50 lbs.) that are normally allowed on international flights. I've known many people who have flown to China with checked bags that weighed 23 kilograms, the limit for international flights, only to be charged a fee once they switch to a domestic flight that only allows 20 kilograms. Frankly, unless you're moving to China, there shouldn't be a need to travel with two checked bags that weigh 50 pounds.

For any domestic Chinese flight that lasts over two hours, it's customary to serve free drinks and a meal, a practice that has all but died in the Western world. The quality of the food isn't terribly high, however, so don't say I didn't warn you.

Buying Chinese Flight Tickets

The process of purchasing a flight ticket in China isn't complicated, and I've already covered the basics earlier. The important point to remember is that when you're doing your research on flights, make sure you get quotes from both international Online Travel Agencies (OTAs) like Expedia, Orbitz, Kayak, etc., as well as Chinese-based OTAs like Ctrip/Trip.

International flights are often priced the same, but domestic flights can have a 10%-20% difference. It is worth at least price comparing:

www.travelchinacheaper.com/try/trip

Once you've purchased your ticket, you can proceed to the airport with only your passport in hand just as you would at home. You don't need to have a printout or confirmation number, although it certainly wouldn't hurt in case of any issues. You'll receive a paper ticket at the check-in counter, and it will read exactly like you expect any airline ticket to read.

Note For those flying with a lap infant, you are still required to purchase a ticket for the infant. Since this can't be done online, you'll need to either call the airline directly, arrange the ticket through a travel agent, or purchase the ticket once you arrive at the airport. In most cases, the cost of an infant ticket is ten percent of the price of a full-fare seat.

Exiting a Chinese Airport

For me, the most stressful part of flying in China is exiting the airport. China has an amazing transportation network, but this can often lead to confusion at an airport. For example, I recently landed at the Shanghai airport and was met with signs for the following transportation options right outside the baggage claim: taxis, buses, shuttles, ride-sharing, the parking lot, a subway, and a maglev.

Unless you have somebody meeting you at the airport, I recommend you determine transportation prior to arrival. If you're taking the subway, figure out which lines you need to take and what stop you'll get off on. If you're taking the taxi, have the address of your hotel ready to give to them. If you're taking a shuttle or a bus, research ahead of time to find which one you need to take.

There will likely be people waiting to pounce on you outside baggage claim: a foreign traveler who looks slightly confused. They'll ask you where you want to go and tell you about their taxi service. It all sounds good, but these are often the places where travelers get ripped off the most. Every airport in China has a designated taxi stand, and this is always the best place to start looking for a legitimate taxi.

Pro Tips for Flying in China

Here are a few tips that I've picked up from flying in and around China over the past decade:

- **Utilize Frequent Flyer Programs**: If you're a frequent flyer, check to see if your home airline is part of an alliance with a Chinese airline. Partner airlines usually honor frequent flyer status which will give you access to VIP check-in, faster security lanes, and airport lounges. Personally, I'm a member of Delta's SkyMiles program, so each time I fly with China Southern, which is also part of the Sky Team alliance, I provide my Delta frequent flyer number. By doing so, I get the perks of any status I have, and I earn miles for my Delta account.
- **Bring Your Own Food**: Subway sandwiches (the U.S.A. fast food chain) are a personal favorite of mine. I prefer to purchase my food prior to boarding the plane so that I don't have to eat what they serve. The only problem is that many Chinese airports don't have great food options to choose from inside the airport, so you'll need to think ahead, especially if it's a smaller airport.
- **Bring Your Own Entertainment**: Naturally, Chinese airlines tend to play Chinese movies or offer Chinese magazines during the flight. If you want to watch anything other than the latest Chinese history or martial

arts film, you'll need to be prepared with your own entertainment.

- **Be Prepared for Delays**: Every airline across the globe experiences delays. I don't deny this. However, my experience in China seems to indicate that Chinese airlines experience them more than most. I've been delayed so many times over the course of my life in China that I now pack my toiletries and an extra pair of underwear in my carry-on. Chinese airlines are very good about arranging hotels in the event of a delay, but you won't get your checked luggage back, so I like to be prepared.

Guide to Taking a Train in China

It doesn't matter if you're taking a high-speed train from Beijing to Shanghai or the slow train from Urumqi to Kashgar, the experience of train travel in China is unforgettable. Although the process of finding the right train, buying tickets, and navigating the station may seem daunting at first, it's thankfully quite predictable and very well-organized. You'll find that train travel in China is one of the fastest, most comfortable, and most reliable modes of transportation in China.

Even if it's faster to fly, I highly recommend you try the train at least once during your travels.

Pros and Cons of Taking a Train in China

There are a lot of great reasons to take a train in China and a few reasons you might want to avoid them. In general, it is my opinion that the pros far outweigh the cons. So, let's take a look at the reasons that trains in China are such a popular form of transportation for travelers.

- **Trains are Usually Cheaper**. In many cases, taking a train in China is the cheapest form of transportation.

Cases where this might not be true is when taking a high-speed train over long distances. If you're seriously looking to save money, buying a hard seat or standing ticket is dirt-cheap despite being incredibly uncomfortable. The best part about buying train tickets is that the prices don't fluctuate like flights do. They're set, so you know exactly how much you'll have to pay.

- **Trains are Often Faster**. Taking a train in China can save time over flying or taking a bus. Train stations are conveniently located in the middle of town, as opposed to most Chinese airports which are far outside the city. In addition, you don't have to arrive at a train station hours in advance of your departure like you do with flights. I usually arrive about 30-45 minutes ahead of my departure time. It also helps that Chinese trains are very punctual, unlike flights which experience delays or buses which are subject to traffic conditions.
- **Trains are Comfortable**. Contrary to what you might imagine, trains in China can be very comfortable. As a general rule, you get more leg room in a train, better opportunity to walk around, and there's usually even a restaurant car. Sleeper car beds aren't bad, and the seats in the new high- speed trains are much better than airplanes.
- **Trains Offer Beautiful Scenery**. Trains offer a unique view of the varied China terrain that rolls by your window. You don't get this beautiful view when taking a bus or airplane.

- **Trains Provide Cultural Experiences.** Trains offer a fun cultural experience that is hard to beat. Spending hours with your fellow Chinese passengers, most of whom will be happy to meet you and curious to chat, will provide a window into Chinese culture that you would never have in a bus or airplane. Taking a train in China is even a good opportunity to practice your Mandarin Chinese.

As much as I like to talk up the advantages of taking a train during your trip through China, there are a few things you should be warned about before taking a train:

- **Trains Can Get Crowded.** This is especially true over the holidays. Trains sell standing tickets that can make the cheaper, lower class seats uncomfortable when they're full of people standing everywhere.
- **Trains Aren't Always Cheaper.** Always do your homework. There are many times where flights have been discounted so heavily that it has been cheaper for me to fly than take a train.
- **Train Tickets Regularly Sell Out.** Because train tickets are put on sale 60 days prior to departure date and prices don't fluctuate, buying a last-minute train ticket can be difficult. As a general rule, I try to buy my China train tickets at least five days prior to departure (much earlier for the Chinese holiday season). Anything sooner than that, and I risk having to buy either a super-expensive business class or an uncomfortable standing ticket.

- **Train Stations Don't Always Cater to Foreigners**. At least not as much as airports do. Many of the older train stations can be confusing for somebody who doesn't speak a bit of Mandarin. Never fear, though! I'll help you navigate the train station below.

Understanding China Train Designations

What most travelers don't know is that you can tell a lot about your Chinese train by looking at the train route number (e.g. "D2847" vs "K1128"). Not only can you determine the speed of your train, it's also usually a good indicator of comfort. In other words, it's good information to have!

The Chinese train is broken down into different categories, which I'll list starting from the fastest/most comfortable down to the slowest/least comfortable:

China's High-Speed Trains ("G" and "D")

Over the past decade, China has invested heavily in its network of high-speed railways and has plans to continue this investment into the foreseeable future. The high-speed rail is divided into two categories: "G" and "D". Aside from the speed and an extra class, they're more similar than they are different. Both categories usually have Western (e.g. seated) toilets as well as power plugs on most first-class seats and all business class and premium seats.

- G – The "G" train, short for "Gaotie" which means "high speed train," is the newest, fastest, and usually the most comfortable Chinese train. It's also the most expensive. These trains usually run at speeds of up to 300 kilometers per hour and are quickly becoming the future of train travel in China. You can purchase second class, first class, and Business class tickets on this train.
- D – The "D" train, short for "Dongche", is often identical to the G train with one exception: speed. These trains don't exceed 250 km/hr. Still, they're comfortable and along certain routes don't add that much more time than the G train. You can purchase first-class and second-class tickets on this train.

China's Standard Trains

Standard trains are the older version of China's rail system and rarely exceed 140 kilometers per hour. Although less common than they used to be before the high-speed train came into existence, you'll still find these standard trains going to smaller cities or throughout less-developed regions of China. Usually, these trains are divided into "Soft Sleeper", "Hard Sleeper", "Hard Seat" and sometimes a "Soft Seat". They don't always have a Western toilet or air conditioning, but they are cheaper.

- Z – The "Z" train is an overnight express train that only runs select routes based on demand. They aren't common, but it's usually the fastest of the "standard" Chinese trains – up to 160km/hr.
- T – The "T" train is short for "Tekuai" which means "Express Train". These trains are usually special routes between two major cities that run faster than other standard trains because they don't have many stops in between. The T trains are also less likely to have sleeper options and are more often divided into first- and second-class sections similar to the D train. High speed of 140 kilometers per hour.
- K – The "K" train is short for "Kuaiche" which simply means "Fast Train." These used to be the most common (and fastest) trains in China before the era of the high-speed train took over. They travel all throughout China between the different provinces.
- Only Numbers – These number trains don't have a letter before them and are considered "ordinary" trains. If the train begins with 1, 2, 4 or 5, it will be slightly faster than a train whose number begins with 6, 7, 8 or 9. The highest speed of these trains is 100-120 kilometers per hour.

- Other – You may also happen to run across an "L" (temporary train during peak season), a "Y" (tourism) and an "S" (train connecting a city with its suburbs) train, but these are much less common.

What to Expect Inside a Chinese Train

To help you understand what to expect when traveling by train in China, allow me to spend some time describing the interior of both the high-speed and standard trains.

For high-speed trains, the two most common ticket classes you can purchase are a first-class seat or a second-class seat. The difference between the two usually has to do with the size of the seat as well as the personal space allowed. The first-class cars are arranged with two seats on either side of a center aisle. Leg room is plentiful and there are often electrical outlets to plug in your electronic device (although this isn't always the case).

The second-class cars have a tighter seating arrangement with three seats on one side of the aisle and two on the other. Leg room feels more like airplane seating, but the seats are still relatively comfortable. I've seen some second-class seats that have electrical outlets, but this is the exception.

Beyond the first- and second-class cars, there are some high-speed trains that offer a Business Class option. These comfortable, reclining leather chairs are a treat for any traveler. Beware, though: it's almost guaranteed to be more expensive than flying to your destination!

Finally, and somewhat less-common, there are a few high-speed Chinese trains which have a super-luxurious class that goes by different names: VIP, Deluxe, Premium, Superior, etc. These tickets are extremely expensive and usually offer private accommodation on the train, sometimes with your own private bathroom.

China's high-speed overnight trains offer the added luxury of a bed. The most common is lined on both sides with private bunks in two layers. Each compartment has its own light, window, and electrical plug.

In my opinion, second-class seats on a high-speed train are comfortable enough for most people and are a great way to save money. However, I find that first-class offers the perfect blend of price and comfort. Plus, I like to work while traveling, so I prefer having elbow room and a plug at my seat.

China's standard trains are broken out into a completely different set of classes. First, you have the Hard Seat cars (Yingzuo) that have, as you would expect, hard bench seats set at a 90-degree angle with a table in between.

For short rides, this is not a bad option; however, it can become incredibly uncomfortable for rides longer than a few hours. There are no electrical outlets and little room for luggage.

A limited number of trains include a Soft Seat car (Ruanzuo) whose seats would more resemble an airplane economy class, albeit a bit less comfortable. You have more personal space and the ability to slightly recline if you like.

The next step up on the average Chinese train are the Hard Sleeper cars (Yingwo), which have berths of six beds (three on each side) with a small table between and no door. These are the tickets which sell out fastest because they are the best mix of price and comfort.

The beds in the hard sleepers aren't extremely comfortable, but at least you can lay down! These seats are designated as "Shangpu" (Top bunk, cheapest), "Zhongpu" (Middle bunk), and "Xiapu" (Lower bunk, most expensive). If you decide to take the top bunk, make sure you feel up to climbing a tiny ladder to get there!

Finally, the best tickets you can buy on the average Chinese train (T, K, P, or L) are known as Soft Sleepers (Ruanwo), whose berths are comprised of four comfortable beds with a door that closes. In the newer trains, these berths even include a small TV and electrical outlets for your computer and phone.

Beds in the soft sleepers are good, but the price can sometimes rival that of an airline ticket. These tickets are designated as "Shangpu" (Top bunk, cheaper) and "Xiapu" (Bottom bunk, slightly more expensive).

Bathrooms on most regular-speed Chinese trains are squatty toilets and often they are not that clean. The only exception is in the soft sleeper car, where there is usually one Western-style toilet.

On most trains you're also likely to find a restaurant car where you can sit down for a meal that can be good but is likely a bit pricey. Feel free to walk around and ask for a menu here. They won't let you sit at the tables unless you order, however, so unfortunately you can't use this as a free place to get away. Trust me...I've tried.

Navigating a Chinese Train Station

When talking to most travelers, they tell me that the Chinese train stations scare them. I get it: they do seem intimidating with their massive labyrinths of halls, stalls, and waiting areas. It's easier than it seems, though. Every train station in China is different, and the newer stations are likely to have more signs in English for you. Still, there is a basic process to a China train station you should understand:

- **Step 1: Get Your Ticket**. I'll go into more detail below on how to buy Chinese train tickets, but for now you should know that every train station has what they call a "Ticket Hall". Usually this ticket hall is outside the main entrance to the station and requires you to pass through its own security check to enter.

- **Step 2: Show Your Ticket**. As you enter the main station, one of the first lines you'll stand in will be the ticket check where you will need to present both your ticket and your passport. The agent checks to make sure that your identity on the two are matching.
- **Step 3: Security Checkpoint**. Your next step is the security checkpoint. This is usually the choke point for any train station, but thankfully it's not as bad as airport security. You should keep your shoes and belt on, and put your luggage through the scanner. Once you walk through a metal detector prepare for a quick but harmless pat down by a security guard.
- **Step 4: Find Your Waiting Hall**: Don't be afraid to find somebody who looks like they work there, show them your ticket and give a questioning look. Almost 90 percent of the time they'll point you in the right direction. If you read Chinese, there should be a board that will display your train number (which you can find on your train ticket) followed by the number of the waiting hall or gate from which you'll depart.
- **Step 5: Board Your Train**: Somewhere between 15-20 minutes before the departure time of your train, the doors will open, and stewards will check your ticket one last time as you head to the train platform. Just follow everybody else, and if you're still confused, find somebody and show them your ticket.

- **Step 6: Enjoy the Ride!** You'll be asked to show your ticket while on the train and sometimes even after you depart, so keep it handy.

When preparing to travel by train in China, it's a good idea to stock up on food and water prior to arriving at the train station. Unlike airports, you may take liquids and food through security with you. I also make sure that all my devices are fully charged since it's nearly impossible to find an electrical outlet at most Chinese train stations.

How to Buy China Train Tickets Online

The best part about modern-day Chinese train travel is that most of the ticketing has moved online. At this point, you still need a paper ticket in hand to board your train, but thankfully you can book these tickets from the comfort of your home country and pick it up once you arrive in China.

There are three main ways to book your Chinese train tickets while you're planning your trip:

- **12306 Website:** The website 12306.cn is the official China railway website and is the most efficient way to purchase tickets...for Chinese people. Aside from the website being all in Chinese, it also requires a Chinese phone number and a Chinese bank account. They don't accept foreign credit cards right now.

- **3rd Party Providers**: For most travelers, this will be your only option, but thankfully it's not a bad one. Third-party providers like China Highlights not only allow you to purchase tickets in English and use your foreign credit card, they'll also arrange to have the tickets delivered to your hotel for you! There's a fee involved, of course, but usually it's only a few dollars per ticket. Check train schedules on their website:

www.travelchinacheaper.com/try/china-highlights-trains

It is possible to purchase Chinese train tickets up to 60 days in advance of your departure, and I highly recommend you take advantage of this advance purchase window. Buying tickets in the station ticket hall is both time consuming and difficult, particularly if you don't have a solid command of the Chinese language.

Once you've purchased tickets online, you can either have them delivered to your hotel room through a third-party provider, or you can pick them up yourself. I pick up my tickets at an official train ticket office (火车票代售点 or "Huo Che piao dai shou dian") which is located throughout every city in China. It usually costs about five renminbi for them to print your ticket, but it is completely worth skipping the hassle at the train station. Otherwise, you'll need to wait in line at the train station ticket hall.

If you're picking up tickets purchased online, make sure you bring your passport and the reference code you were given when the tickets were purchased. It's a ten-digit code that begins with one letter and ends in nine numbers (e.g. “E123456789”).

How to Buy China Train Tickets at the Station

Before we return to the train station, let me say that even if you don’t buy Chinese train tickets online, it’s possible to use the official train ticket office I just mentioned in the section above to purchase tickets in person. There’s a five-renminbi surcharge, but there usually isn’t any line.

If, for one reason or another, you must purchase your tickets at the train station, make sure you arrive with your passport and cash. If you’re purchasing for multiple people, you’ll need to have their passports as well.

It’s always best to approach the agent with a Plan A, Plan B and Plan C in case you don’t get what you want. I would even recommend that you have it written down for convenience. For instance, let’s say you want to go from Beijing to Shanghai on Friday. Your Plan A might be first-class tickets on Friday; in case that’s sold out, Plan B might be a different time on Friday; if even that’s not available, Plan C would be to consider second-class or a different day altogether.

This “Plan A, B, C” method is important because there’s nothing worse than waiting in line only to have your plans foiled with no backup. You must leave the window, regroup with your fellow travelers, and stand in line again. I’ve done that before, and it is frustrating.

China Trains · Frequently Asked Questions

The following are the most common questions I hear about train travel in China:

- **What are the luggage restrictions on a Chinese train?** Officially there are luggage weight and size limits, but they're never enforced. If you can carry it on your person and it fits through a scanning machine, it will be permitted. The only thing to consider is that there's no such thing as "checked baggage" on a train. You must carry and store it by your seat, and often there's not a lot of room to do so. In general, there's more space in first-class, business class, and a soft sleeper, and less room to store luggage in the second-class, hard sleeper, and hard seat cars.
- **How far in advance can I purchase train tickets?** Train tickets can be purchased 60 days in advance of the scheduled departure date.
- **Can train tickets be transferred, changed or returned for a refund?** No, yes, and yes. Let me explain. No, you can't transfer your ticket because it is attached to your passport number. What you can do is return the tickets or have them changed, although it's not the easiest process. If you purchased your tickets online through 12306.cn, you can change or return the tickets from there as long as you haven't already picked up a printed ticket. Otherwise, you'll need to make the change in person at the ticket hall. Don't forget to bring the original ticket and your passport!

- **Can I get off the train during stops?** Getting off the train during stops used to be common but is now highly discouraged. More than likely the train stewardess won't let you leave unless it's your stop.
- **How will I know when to get off the train if I can't speak Chinese?** After getting on the train, a steward/stewardess will come and check your ticket, making note of where you're getting off. At each stop, he or she will come down the aisles calling out the name of the station and, in the case of most foreign travelers, will come and tell you that it is your stop.
- **Can I bring food onto the train?** Yes, you can! In fact, I highly recommend bringing food since the food on the train isn't that good and is overpriced. Both food and drink are welcome on a Chinese train.

Pro Tips for Chinese Train Travel

As somebody who has taken every type of China train to every size of China train station over the past ten years, I've learned a thing or two about how to make the best of the experience. This is something I hope to be able to pass on to you. The following are a few of the "pro tips" I've picked up over the years:

- If you don't know a lick of Mandarin, download China Highlight's China Train Booking app (available on Apple iOS and Android). It's possible to purchase tickets through the app, but I find it equally useful for planning, letting you know what trains run on what days and approximately how many tickets are available. **Note:** *If you can read Mandarin, the 12306 app does the same thing but is more up-to-date.*

- When picking your tickets, I recommend the middle bunk (中铺 or "Zhongpu") of a hard sleeper train or the top bunk (上铺 or "Shangpu") of the soft sleeper train. The bottom bunks always have people sitting on them during the day and the top bunk of the hard sleeper has too little room between the bed and the train car ceiling.
- Bring hand sanitizer, particularly for longer trips.
- Bring a small book light if you like to read. Once the lights go out at night during an overnight train, you're on your own.
- If you're not sure you'll have a plug to charge your phone on a long journey, buy an external battery pack before you leave. They're cheap and they'll give you an extra full battery charge or two.
- Noise cancelling headphones are great on airplanes. They're *priceless* on a China train – I never leave home without mine!
- When you get off the train and out of the station, you're probably going to be mobbed by people yelling "Taxi!" Ignore them. Every train station has a place for official taxis to wait, and if you can't find the location, just walk to the nearest major street and wait for a taxi. The hawkers you meet will always charge you far more than you should pay and usually aren't even legal.

- Bring your own entertainment. Download movies, take along a card deck, or whatever else you like. You're probably not going to like any movie that might be shown on the train (if there even is one).

Guide to Using Taxis in China

Taxis are ubiquitous in China. They're usually fast, comfortable, and quite cheap, at least when compared to their Western counterparts. You'll recognize Chinese taxis by their bright colors (usually green, yellow or red) in addition to the sign on top of the vehicle and the LED light on the front dash.

Taxis vary from city to city in China, including both the condition of the vehicle and the price at which the fare begins.

In many cities, there are general places that are easier to get taxis than others, such as in front of a hotel, but all you need to do is to stand by the side of the road and wave your hand to alert an empty taxi to pull over. They'll stop almost anywhere to pick you up.

At this point you'll always want to enter the taxi from the passenger side. The driver will ask you where you want to go and then drop the meter to start your fare once you begin moving. There's a display somewhere on the car dashboard that will tell you exactly how much your fare is at that moment, and when you stop to get out, that's exactly what you should be charged. You're not expected to tip the driver at all and frankly it would be weird to do so.

Note: If the taxi must pay any road fees, including fees to exit the airport or tolls on the road, those fees will generally be added to your fare.

The key to successfully navigating the China taxi system is to come prepared. Before you even step foot inside the taxi there are a couple things you might want to have with you:

- **Cash**: I haven't seen a single Chinese taxi that accepts credit cards. There are a number that accept mobile payments like WeChat and Alipay, but in the end, cash is king.
- **Your Destination**: If you don't speak Mandarin very well, you'll want to have the name of the place you're going written down on a piece of paper. Most hotels and hostels can help you by writing down your destination in Chinese characters, and you'll want to pick up a card in the hotel lobby that says the name and address of that hotel. When entering the taxi, just hand the card over, and they'll know where to go from there.

Black Taxis and Ride Sharing

There are certain times of the day, particularly during rush hour, when taxis are difficult to come by, and you might find cars passing by flashing their lights at you. These are what's known as "black taxis", and although they might not always be black in color, they can be quite handy.

When a black taxi slows and rolls down their window, you're expected to tell them where you want to go. At that point the driver either agrees to take you there or decides it's not the direction he wants to head. That's a big difference between a legitimate taxi and a black taxi: legitimate taxis are required to take you where you want to go; black taxi can deny you service.

The next part is very important: you need to negotiate price prior to starting the ride in a black taxi. I've been in too many situations where the price hadn't been properly negotiated, and I either ended up arguing with the driver or paying a much higher price than I should have. All of that can be avoided by negotiating price beforehand.

Another popular taxi option is the Chinese equivalent to Uber known as "Didi Chuxing". Didi is an app that can be downloaded to your phone that allows you to input your destination and call for a driver. It's not available in every Chinese city yet, but it's spreading quickly.

The Didi app has an English version, which is convenient, and allows for mobile payment via WeChat, Alipay and even Apple Pay. The catch here is that you're required to have a working phone number. Drivers will use this phone number to call you prior to pick-up, so if you're not prepared to speak Chinese, this option might not work well for you.

Tips for Using Taxis in China

Here are a few final tips to consider when taking taxis in China:

- Make sure the driver starts the meter. This is especially true when exiting the airport, train station, or bus station. Some drivers will try to take advantage of you and "bargain" a price with you. This is illegal, and you'll probably get ripped off if you do so. Make sure they "drop the flag" on the dashboard meter to start your service.
- Pay Using Small Bills: If your fare is ten renminbi, don't give the driver a 100-renminbi bill. Many travelers have reported receiving fake bills in return, and sometimes drivers won't even have the correct amount of change.
- Don't Tip the Driver: This isn't a custom in China, and he's not expecting it, even from foreign travelers. Just say 'thank you' and be on your way.
- Keep the Receipt: You might want to keep your receipt at least a day or two. Why? The receipt has the vehicle number, so that if you happen to lose your wallet or other valuable in the car, you can have your hotel call up and locate the exact taxi driver to return your belongings.

Guide to Taking a Bus in China

When it comes to traveling in China, most tourists opt to either fly or hop on a train. The reasoning is quite simple: flying is fast, and trains are cheap. There are times, however, when China's massive, intercity bus system is your best option. Perhaps the flights are too expensive, or the train is too full. Maybe you want to save a few dollars, or you're heading to a place that isn't serviced by an airport or train station.

Whatever the reason, if you plan to take a bus in China, you'll want to familiarize yourself with the process of buying tickets and boarding your bus.

Pros and Cons of Bus Travel in China

There are a number of reasons why you might want to take a bus in China, as well as a few reasons you would potentially want to avoid it. Over the decade, I've seen my fair share of both while traveling on a Chinese bus. Let's start by breaking down a few of the reasons that a bus is a good option for tourists:

- **Frequency**: Chinese buses often run at a higher frequency than flights or trains in China. Most of the time you don't have to worry about booking in advance because there will be a bus between two cities that runs every 20-30 minutes.

- **Convenience**: Compared to Chinese airports and train stations, security at a bus station is a breeze. I rarely arrive at a bus station any earlier than 30 minutes before my departure, and I still end up waiting for 15 minutes.
- **Station Location**: Most of the time Chinese bus stations are in the heart of a city as opposed to airports which are usually on the edge of town. This can not only save you time, but it also saves you the expense of a taxi into town.
- **Availability**: I have never bought a bus ticket earlier than a day in advance, and often I buy it on the day of departure. Unlike flights and trains, China bus tickets tend to have more availability, giving you the flexibility to change your itinerary at a moment's notice.

That's what makes China bus travel good. Here's a bit of what I don't like about China bus travel:

- **Unreliable Comfort**: Sometimes you can get lucky and board a relatively new bus, but more often than not, you'll find yourself riding a vehicle that has seen a couple decades' worth of use. It's a gamble you take, and sometimes it can be quite uncomfortable.
- **Unreliable Delays**: Unexpected delays are possible no matter what form of transportation you decide to take. Unlike planes and trains, buses usually leave right on time. The difficulty comes with the unpredictability of

the roads. I have been stuck in horrendous city traffic for hours, my bus has been stopped on the highway for a security checkpoint, my bus has broken down, and I've run into road construction delays. It isn't fun, but there's nothing you can do about it.

- **A Different Kind of Traveler**: Buses are the poor man's transportation; there's just no way around it. Don't get me wrong, the people are great, but since it's not a high-profile means of transportation, the rules don't always get enforced. Smoking is a great example: it's common to see people smoking on a bus despite numerous signs saying it is forbidden. I've also seen a man walk onto a bus carrying a car windshield. I'm not joking! Needless to say, his seat mate was miserable during the entire ride. These kinds of things technically aren't permitted, but the rules are much more relaxed on Chinese buses.

Hopefully I haven't discouraged you from attempting to take a bus in China; I just want to make sure you have a dose of reality. There are plenty of good reasons to take a bus (and I hope you do), but make sure you set your expectations before buying your ticket.

What to Expect · A Chinese Bus

If you've never had a chance to look inside a Chinese bus, and you're afraid about what you're getting into, allow me to walk you through the average bus. Generally, there are two basic kinds of buses in China: the seated bus and the sleeper bus.

The seated bus is exactly what it sounds like. There are usually two sets of two seats with a middle aisle and all the seats facing toward the front of the bus. As a tall guy, I've never had a complaint about the leg room in a Chinese bus, but the seats can be somewhat narrow. Buses usually have an entertainment system that will play Chinese movies throughout the duration of the journey, and most buses have an air-conditioning and heating system. Your seat will recline slightly, but don't expect a great sleeping position. A few seated buses have a bathroom, but often they won't be open for passengers. Even if they were, you might not want to use them unless it's an absolute emergency.

All seats in a seated bus are priced equally and are sold on a first-come-first-served basis. Thankfully, prices don't fluctuate like airline tickets do.

A sleeper bus is different: travelers each have a bed instead of a seat. There are usually three rows of beds with two aisles in between and a bathroom toward the back. There is a top and bottom bed the entire length of the bus. Anybody whose height exceeds five feet eight inches will have trouble fitting onto one of these beds, as do I. I don't have the option to hang my feet over the edge since that is somebody else's bed, so I end up having to scrunch up a little.

These buses also usually have an entertainment system, air conditioning, and heating, although it all depends on the age of the bus you are riding. Beds are priced higher for the top bunk than the bottom bunk in a sleeper bus.

Arriving at the Chinese Bus Station

To the unseasoned China traveler, it seems simple enough to find a bus station. It should be easy, right? Pull out your handy Mandarin phrasebook, look up "bus station" and tell the taxi driver where you want to go. Boom! You're done.

Unfortunately, it's not always that easy. Except for small towns, most cities in China have a number of different bus stations scattered around. One may be a "long distance bus station" while the other is an "International Bus Station." Often, bus stations are categorized by which direction on the compass their buses head or even by which specific city or region they service. The bottom line is that the word "bus station" just doesn't cut it. You need to know exactly which bus station you want to go to. How do you do this? Here are a couple ways:

- **Refer to Travel Guide Books.** Good China travel guide books will give details on which bus stations go to which cities.
- **Ask Your Hotel or Hostel.** It is possible your hotel won't know off-hand, but they'll be able to ask the appropriate people and then write down the name of the bus station on a piece of paper which you can hand to your taxi driver.

- **Ask Your Taxi Driver.** Don't just tell the taxi driver to head to a bus station. Instead, tell him specifically which city you're taking a bus to. In many cases, a taxi driver will know where you should go.

How to Find a Chinese Bus Schedule

In my opinion, the most confusing part about taking an intra-city bus in China is figuring out the schedule. Unlike trains and airplanes, it's much harder to check schedules or even buy tickets online.

For most major intra-city connections, China buses commonly depart once every twenty minutes, half-hour or hour. There are some cities where only a handful or even one or two buses depart each day. In this case you'll want to have an idea of the bus schedule.

Most bus stations either post their schedule on the wall or have an LED board that lists destinations and departures to each city. Sometimes they are translated into English, but often they are not, so the ability to read Chinese characters is required.

For those who can't read Chinese characters, the best thing you can do is visit the bus ticket counter with your desired destination in hand. They'll ask you what date you want to leave and show you the options on the computer screen.

How to Buy Bus Tickets

Since buying bus tickets online has not quite taken off yet, you're left with only two options: buy a ticket at the bus station or have a proxy do it for you.

China now runs on a "real-name ticket system" for all transportation, including buses, which means that you must have an official form of identification, such as a passport, in order to purchase bus tickets. Once your ticket is purchased, you can't transfer this ticket to anybody else without returning it and buying a new one.

Standing in line at a Chinese bus station isn't my favorite activity in the world, but it's usually not as bad as standing in line at a train station. Most of the time I arrive on my day of departure, stand in line, and purchase a ticket. You'll want to have cash ready for the purchase since bank cards usually aren't accepted, particularly foreign credit cards.

There are many Chinese hostels that will offer a ticket purchasing service for guests. You would need to provide a photocopy of your passport, and they'll charge you a fee, but at least you don't have to stand in line yourself.

China Buses · Frequently Asked Questions

Here are the most common questions I receive about taking buses in China:

- **What can you take on a bus?** The beauty of the Chinese bus is that you can take almost anything you want. People take bicycles, overweight pieces of luggage, instruments...you name it. There isn't an official weight limit, so whatever can easily fit in the underneath hatch is usually permitted.
- **What are you prohibited from taking on a bus?** Like any other form of transportation in China, there are still some things that you can't take with you through the security checkpoint of the bus station: knives, bottles of any kind of liquid, fuel canisters used for camping, lighters, etc. For drinks, you can buy water and sodas at shops inside the bus station.
- **Can you smoke on a China bus?** While officially prohibited, unfortunately I've seen plenty of passengers and even bus drivers smoke on a bus. Most people wait for a rest stop to pull out their cigarettes, but that's not always the case. If you don't like smoking, it's not impolite to ask the smoker next to you to put out their cigarette. Be bold! You're a foreigner, and you can get away with it.
- **Are there electrical outlets or Wi-Fi on a China bus?** No. I wish there were, but I have yet to see a seated or a sleeper bus with electrical outlets or Wi-Fi.
- **Can I get off anywhere along the bus route?** Yes, you can. Just tell the driver exactly where you want to get off, such as a specific village or place along the road. The driver will alert you when you arrive and will stop to let you off.

- **Do buses pick up hitchhikers in China?** Yes, they do. If you're out in the boondocks, you can stand on the side of the road and try to wave down a bus. They won't stop if they're full, but if they stop, just tell them where you're going on and hop on. You'll have to pay the driver directly, and they're usually pretty good about giving a fair price for transport.

Pro Tips for Bus Travel in China

Over the many years that I've taken buses across China, there are a few quick tips I've picked up that I believe could be helpful to you or even save you money:

- **Take the Night Bus.** Want to save some money? Take the night sleeper bus to save yourself the money of a hotel. It won't be as comfortable of a sleep, but you'll manage, I promise.
- **Take Your Own Food.** The rest stops for buses can be sketchy at best. Food options are limited, and the hole-in-the-wall restaurants are usually a recipe for disaster. Stock up on food before you leave to make sure you can survive on what you have in your own bag.
- **Keep Valuables with You.** While I recommend you store your luggage in the lower storage compartments, make sure you have all your valuables with you at your seat. I've known a couple people who have had items stolen from these lower luggage storage compartments.

- **Bring Your Own Light.** This tip is for the overnight sleeper buses. Sometimes you'll have a light to read by, but many times you won't.

Guide to Renting a Car in China

There are some travelers who prefer the freedom and autonomy of renting their own car. I know, because I'm one of them! I've been driving in China for a number of years now, and although the roads are often scary and confusing, I relish the opportunity to explore the country on my own terms.

Perhaps you're the same way. While the crowded roads in China are usually enough to scare most people away, it's the freedom to explore beyond the city that many crave.

I wish I could tell you that renting a car and driving yourself around the country is going to be easy, but that's just not the Chinese way! It's going to be a challenge no matter who you are, how well you speak Chinese, and how much money you have to spend. Consider the simple fact that China does not accept any international licenses. Not a single one. This means that for you to legally drive in China, you'll either have to visit the Department of Motor Vehicles to take a test to earn your license, or you'll have to apply for a provisional license.

Of course, renting a car with a Chinese driver is a much easier option, albeit more expensive. The benefit of hiring a driver is that they'll know the roads and the burden of liability will rest on them. Driving your own car means that if a wreck occurs, you'll be responsible to work through the mess. Trust me, it's not fun.

There are a few other factors to consider when renting a car to drive in China:

- While some car rental companies accept major credit cards, there are many others that do not, particularly outside of larger Chinese cities. If the company doesn't accept credit cards, you'll be required to put down a sizable cash deposit. At one point, I had to put down about US$1,000 in cash to rent a car out in the western region of Xinjiang.
- If you're paying with cash, car rental companies will have to hold back about 2,000 RMB for 30 days after you drop off the car. They do this in case a traffic ticket gets reported. I had to pick up my security deposit personally, but they can direct deposit this money into a Chinese bank account if you have one.
- Many rental cars have distance limits. Some limit you to 300 kilometers per day, which isn't much if you're driving between cities.
- Parking is a nightmare and is usually very costly. Most hotels will charge you an extra fee to keep your car parked overnight.

You'll be able to find car rental companies at most major airports in China, although they're not nearly as prevalent as they are in the West. You'll want to look for the small offices outside baggage claim before you exit the terminal. Honestly, going this route is a bit of a gamble because I've spoken with some rental companies that won't accept credit cards and others won't rent to foreign travelers.

To eliminate the uncertainty, you can also contact travel agencies in China to request a "self-drive tour". This is how the Chinese people usually think of car rentals. In this way, you can know for certain that you've booked a car prior to your arrival and where you can pick it up. I recommend asking for pictures of the exact car you're renting prior to providing a down payment. Travel agencies are also a good place to inquire about provisional Chinese driver's licenses.

Guide to Bike Rentals in China

Once you start walking around most major Chinese cities, it will be hard to ignore the thousands of colorful bicycles that line the streets on either side. China has thoroughly embraced the idea of bike sharing, and these cheap but convenient bikes are everywhere.

As somebody who has lived many years in China, I can tell you that these bikes can be extremely convenient. A simple bike can turn a long 30-minute walk from the subway station into a quick five-minute ride. Best of all, there's no need to worry about anybody stealing your bike. You just scan the bike to unlock it and then lock it up whenever you reach your destination.

There is only one (somewhat big) problem: they've historically been difficult for tourists to use.

In order to unlock one of these bike-share bikes, there have been two important requirements:

- **A Mobile Phone**: In order to unlock and use these bikes, you need a phone that has a mobile network connection. There are a number of ways to do this, all of which I will cover in the next chapter about setting up a mobile phone in China.

- **A Method of Payment**: This is the one that trips up most tourists. It used to be that a Chinese bank account was required in order to pay for these bike shares. Thankfully, there are alternative methods for international travelers.

Mobike is an excellent example. You can download the Mobike app in your own country and attach it to your own bank account before you leave for China. You can use the app while in China, and the charges will be made in the currency of the country where the account is registered. Mobike converts the payment automatically.

While you'll be restricted to only one bike-share option (and it only works if you have a network connection on your phone), I'm happy to say there is a way to use bike-share bikes in China.

Step 5:

STAYING CONNECTED IN CHINA

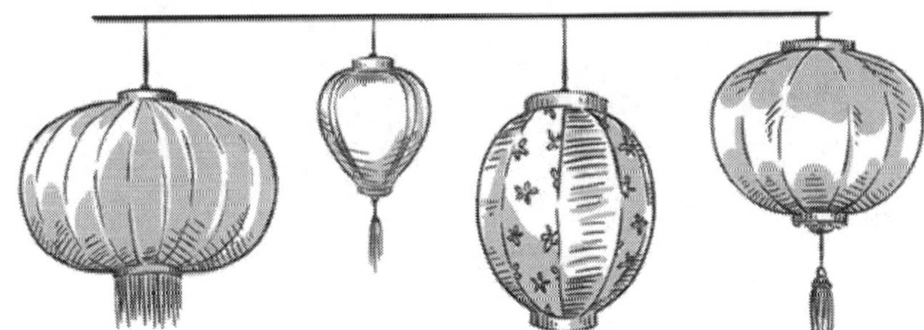

Setting up a Mobile Phone in China

It's hard to imagine a time when travelers weren't so reliant on our cell phones! They are our maps, our translators, and our only connection to people back home. At this point in time, losing my phone would cause more headaches than losing my wallet!

Some people are perfectly content (if not happy) to leave their phones behind as they travel the world. If that's you, I commend you.

For the majority of us, however, that's just not possible. So, what are your options with regard to using a cell phone in China? There are four primary ways to maintain a cell phone connection while traveling China:

1. **Bring your own phone on your own plan**. Although this is the most expensive option, it's also the easiest. Most carriers offer international plans that include some combination of text, data, and/or calls. The moment you land in China, your phone will immediately connect to a local Chinese carrier, and you will be charged based on the rates the carrier in your home country sets. If you don't want to be charged, make sure you take the

Subscriber Identification Module (SIM) card out of your phone prior to landing in China.

2. **Bring your own phone, buy a Chinese SIM card**. The cheaper option is to buy a Chinese SIM card once you arrive in China, and insert it into your current phone. Phone and data rates are dirt cheap in China, but you might run into two big problems here. First, your cell phone needs to be unlocked, which must be done by your carrier once you've paid off the phone. Second, purchasing a SIM card can be a troublesome ordeal which involves registering the SIM card with your passport. It's not difficult, but it takes time.

3. **Rent a phone and SIM card**. There are services that allow you to rent a phone and SIM card to be delivered to your home prior to departing for China. In this way, you'll have a phone to use the moment you land without compromising the security of your personal phone by connecting it to Chinese networks. Learn more about renting a phone in China here:

   www.travelchinacheaper.com/try/phone-rental

4. **Use Only Wi-Fi**. Of course, the cheapest option is to bring your own phone and only use Wi-Fi. This is what a lot of budget travelers do, and it works for the most part, but it's becoming more difficult as China attempts to monitor all user activity online. This means that to use free Wi-Fi at places such as an airport, train station, or coffee house, you'll need to identify yourself by providing a code sent as a text to your Chinese cell phone number. Since that number should technically be

registered with your identification card, your activity online can now be linked to you. If that sounds a little too "big brother", you can also look into a global Wi-Fi option. They're surprisingly affordable and work well in China. See an example here:

www.travelchinacheaper.com/try/global-wifi

Any of these methods will work, but they each have their pros and cons. Getting a phone with some sort of data plan is only half the battle, though. The next equally difficult challenge is connecting to the uncensored world from within China's borders.

Censorship & the Internet in China

China's active censorship of the internet is often jokingly referred to in English as "The Great Firewall". China has a special department called the Ministry of Information whose specific job is to control the flow of information into and out of China.

Ever since 2009, this control has included completely blocking websites like Facebook, Twitter, Instagram, Gmail, YouTube, and many foreign media outlets.

Much of what you use on your phone right now likely won't work in China without first tunneling under this "Great Firewall" of censorship. The easiest solution to this problem is a service known as a "Virtual Private Network" or "VPN" for short.

If you've never heard of a VPN, I'll share a quick definition. A VPN is a way to encrypt your data by creating a secure connection (or "tunnel") between your computer and a server elsewhere in the world. Its primary purpose is to protect your data from being stolen while it's traveling freely across the internet, but the side benefit is that in places like China, the VPN metaphorically tunnels under The Great Firewall. Instead of viewing the internet as a computer or phone in China, a VPN allows you to see the internet from the perspective of the server you're connecting to. If your VPN connects you to a server in the United States, you'll experience the internet as if you were physically in the country.

The only downside is that using a VPN costs a bit of money and ends up slowing down your internet speeds slightly. You can check out ExpressVPN, the service I recommend to China travelers, here:

www.travelchinacheaper.com/view/expressvpn

Is Using a VPN in China Illegal?

The next logical question that most people ask is whether or not using a VPN is legal. It's an excellent question, and the answer isn't black and white.

VPNs are a necessary part of doing business anywhere in the world. VPNs are used by every major and minor corporation to keep their trade secrets safe. China regulates the use of VPNs for companies operating in China, but they haven't officially regulated it for individual users. They'll often block popular VPN service addresses and make connecting to different servers difficult from within China, but they haven't outright banned VPN use.

The reality is that China doesn't really care if foreigners connect to the internet via a VPN. Their primary concern is making sure that Chinese citizens are kept sheltered by censorship. While there have been reports of Chinese residents getting in trouble for using a VPN, I have yet to hear any reports of foreigners getting into any sort of trouble for using a VPN.

Which VPN is Recommended for China?

If you're like me, you'd like to remain connected to your email and social media at least a little bit while you're traveling. In this case, I highly recommend you purchase a VPN service prior to traveling to China.

Since I live in China and rely on the internet for my business, I keep two active VPN subscriptions at all times for backup. Personally, I use and recommend ExpressVPN and NordVPN, both of which have historically worked well in China. Use the links below to get special discounts on each service should you decide to use one:

- ExpressVPN: www.travelchinacheaper.com/view/expressvpn
- NordVPN: www.travelchinacheaper.com/view/nordvpn

Communicating Back Home from China

One added benefit of our increasingly connected world is the ability to make voice and video phone calls over the internet, avoiding the need for costly international fees or phone charges. On a weekly basis, my family gathers around the computer at our home here in China to call family back home in the United States and for the most part, the connection is good, and the picture is clear.

This type of connection, known as VOIP or "Voice Over Internet Protocol", requires specific software on your phone or computer. I'd like to list out for you a few the more popular options as well as notes on how well they work here in China:

- **Skype**: Skype is probably the most popular VOIP software, but it's been notoriously unreliable here in China. At times it has been blocked and won't connect. In my experience it's always been a poor connection. If you want to use Skype in China, it's best to connect through a VPN.
- **FaceTime**: If you're an Apple user, you're probably familiar with iMessage and FaceTime. In the past, these

services have been blocked but as of the publication of this book, it's been surprisingly reliable. The connection is usually very good but using FaceTime requires both users to be part of the Apple ecosystem.

- **Facebook Messenger and WhatsApp**: Both Messenger and WhatsApp are blocked here in China, so using these services will require a VPN connection.
- **WeChat**: Because it's a Chinese app, WeChat tends to be the most reliable software for voice and video phone calls in China. The benefit of using WeChat is knowing that it will work. The con of the software is that anybody you want to connect with will need to download and register on WeChat, not to mention the fact that WeChat has acknowledged the Chinese government has a backdoor into the system. If you don't mind big brother listening in on your call, WeChat will always be the most reliable option.

Sending & Receiving Mail in China

There are times while traveling around China that you might have a need to send or receive physical mail. Perhaps you want to send a postcard to a family member, or you need to receive some mail from home while you're on the road.

The process to send and receive mail isn't as intimidating as you might think, so I'll ease any anxiety by walking you through the process step-by-step.

How to Send Mail in China

Sending mail in China is as simple as finding a Chinese post office (called a 邮局 or "yóujú") and paying for postage. The typical post card should only cost approximately US$1 to send internationally while prices for packages will naturally vary based on size, weight and destination.

Postage for each postcard, letter or package must be individually purchased, so you can't expect to purchase a sheet of stamps to use when you want. If you're wanting to send postcards or letters in China, I recommend writing them all together and visiting the post office only once.

Important Note: China has a number of interesting restrictions when it comes to items which aren't allowed to be shipped overseas. Aside from banning any material "which involve State secrets" (and what would that be exactly?), you're also banned from mailing out that cool knife you bought. See the entire list of customs regulations here:

www.ems.com.cn/serviceguide/e_you_jian_bao_guan.html

How to Receive Mail in China

As a traveler, it's always a bit tricky to receive mail while you're on the road. If you know a hotel where you're going to stay for an extended period of time, it's possible to give the address for your hotel as your delivery address. There are a few things that you'll need to know before you do this, however.

First, understand that mail delivery in China isn't always reliable. Don't get me wrong, the package will get delivered, but it could take three days, or it could take three weeks. There are no guarantees unless you pay an exorbitant sum for priority delivery from an international logistics company.

Second, to ensure delivery in China, you'll need to provide a phone number. It's best if you list your personal Chinese phone number, but if you don't have that you'll want to get permission to put the phone number of your hotel or hostel. The reason for listing your phone number is that delivery companies always call before making a delivery, and if nobody answers, they often won't deliver.

Special Mail Service for Serial Travelers

I'd like to share one final tip for those of you who are serial travelers or who find themselves constantly on the road. A few years ago, I set up what is known as a virtual address, and it has been amazing for me.

In short, a virtual mailbox is a permanent address in the United States where I have all my mail sent. Once it arrives, the service I use scans the mail and alerts me to new mail. I can then log in on my phone or computer to let them know whether to open the mail, scan the mail, forward the mail, or shred the mail. No matter where I am in the world, I have access to my physical mail and can have it forwarded wherever I want.

I use Traveling Mailbox, which you can learn more about here:

www.travelchinacheaper.com/try/travel-mail

This is a special service that only applies to a small segment of travelers, but if that's you, I promise you this virtual mailbox is a game-changer.

Step 6:

NAVIGATING THE CHINESE LANGUAGE BARRIER

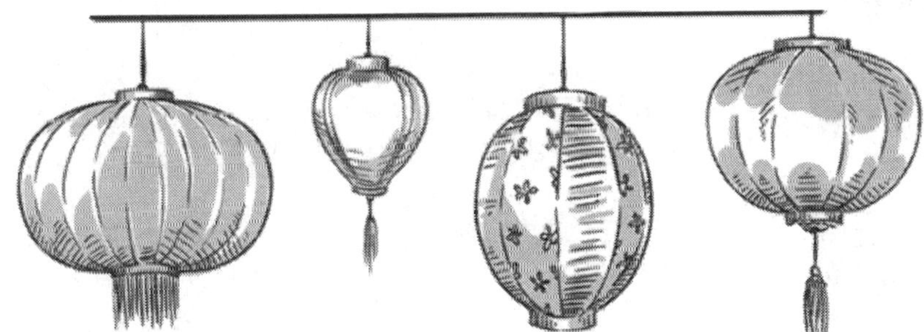

The Chinese Language(s)

As you plan your travel to China, it's quite natural to have concerns about the language. Chinese is routinely listed as one of the most difficult languages to master, and most travelers won't have the time to learn more than a few words or phrases before they arrive. When you combine that with the added difficulty of reading and writing the thousands of Chinese characters, it may seem daunting to attempt to communicate or understand anything while in China.

Thankfully, Chinese people won't expect you to be able to speak Chinese. In fact, most locals here are shocked when they hear me, a tall white foreigner, speak Chinese and are delighted when I make the attempt to communicate in their language. As a traveler, taking the time to learn a few greetings or polite phrases will go a long way in endearing you to the people you meet along the way.

What you'll likely find as you travel around China is that many locals will use English to communicate with you. It may not be fluent, and it may be hard to understand, but it's one option for communication. English classes are a part of the Chinese education system from elementary up to university, and those families with extra money often send their children to English tutoring classes on the weekend.

In this chapter I want to share with you some simple tips for traveling around China if you don't speak Chinese, as well as tips on learning a bit before you leave. First things first, though. I need to explain to you exactly what I mean by "Chinese language."

Mandarin, Cantonese & Chinese Dialects

When I use the term "Chinese language," I am referring to the official language in China, known as "Mandarin Chinese." This is the language that is most commonly associated with China and the one that is spoken by close to 1.2 billion people. That's quite a lot of people when you consider that Spanish is spoken natively by about 400 million people and English by only 360 million!

However, Mandarin Chinese isn't the only language that is spoken in China. The Cantonese language is a language spoken in places like Hong Kong, Macau, and the southern Guangdong province of China. While Cantonese and Mandarin Chinese share a few words and written characters, the two languages are mutually unintelligible. For those who can't speak Cantonese, which includes me, it's good to know that the colonial British roots of Hong Kong and Macau mean that it's quite easy to get around using English.

The most interesting linguistic challenge in China has to do with the various dialects that are used throughout the country.

In addition to the "putonghua" or "standard Chinese" version of the Mandarin language, there's also the Shanghai dialect known as "Shanghai hua," the Sichuan dialect known as "Sichuan hua," the Hakka dialect, Gan dialect, and many, many more. When you factor in the various ethnic groups in China that have their own language, such as the Uyghur, Mongol, and Tibetans, you can see the difficulty one can face with languages while traveling around China.

Don't let this intimidate you, though! If you're going to learn any language for your time in China, you'll want to dedicate your time to studying Mandarin Chinese. If you don't have time to learn Chinese before you travel, then read on.

How to Travel China without Learning Chinese

While I've spent a lot of time and effort personally learning Mandarin, I realize that the majority of travelers will arrive in China not being able to speak more than a word or two of Mandarin Chinese. If that's you, don't fret; you're not alone. Every year, thousands upon thousands of tourists travel to China without speaking even the slightest bit of Chinese.

In fact, I've met quite a few expats in China who have lived here for years and can do nothing more than use a taxi and order food in Chinese. This is especially true in international cities like Beijing and Shanghai which have large expat populations and areas of the city which cater to English-speaking foreigners. When it's too easy to get around in English, there's not as much incentive to persist through the difficulty of learning Chinese.

As you can tell, speaking Mandarin isn't a "must" in order to travel to China. Most major tourist cities are fairly easy to navigate without being able to speak Mandarin Chinese. Taxi drivers are trained to know enough English to get you where you need to go, and many restaurants use written English in addition to pictures on their menus.

The trouble comes when you want to travel outside the city, into the countryside, or anywhere where tourists aren't as common. It's at this point that you need to consider how you'll be able to communicate with those who have absolutely no ability to speak English.

If you don't have the time to learn Mandarin Chinese, but you still want to explore parts of China that go beyond the popular tourist spots, there are still a few options for you to consider. Taking advantage of these options will enhance your visit to China by giving you access to more of the China culture and in many cases earn you the favor of those with whom you speak.

Option #1: Use a Chinese Phrase Guide

The easiest and probably most often utilized fix for not speaking Mandarin Chinese is using a phrase book. Most of them come in pocket-sized editions that are light to carry and simple to use; they cater to those who know very little of the language. In many cases, there will often be a language section in whatever China travel guide book you choose to use.

Here are two of my favorite Mandarin phrase books for you to consider.

- **Lonely Planet Mandarin Phrasebook**: *Lonely Planet* does a good job of giving you the most practical phrases you might want to use as a traveler. Topics include "Sightseeing", "Social", "Emergencies," and "Eating". There is even a menu decoder that is quite useful. This phrase book is offered with an audio CD to help you master the correct pronunciation.

- **The Most Basic Chinese**: This is a great phrasebook for those who plan on taking a longer trip. It's nice because it not only offers downloadable audio files and an e-book option, it is also by far the cheapest phrase book on the market.

If you think that a Mandarin phrase book is what you need, get links to purchase these and other great phrase book options here:

www.travelchinacheaper.com/mandarin-phrasebooks

Option #2 - Use Your Smartphone

You might be surprised at the technology that is available via the small computer in your pocket. Whether you own a phone running Android or Apple iOS, you'll find a number of excellent apps which allow you to get near real-time translations.

Consider the iTranslate app as an example. Once you set up the Mandarin language, all you have to do is speak into your phone, and the app will provide immediate voice translation. It works in reverse as well, where a Chinese person can speak into the phone, and it will dictate the translation to you in English. In my experience, the efficiency of the service is directly related to the speed of the network connection, but Chinese networks are usually very good.

These voice translation apps are an amazing tool, and one I recommend you look into. There are free and paid versions which you can learn more about here:

www.travelchinacheaper.com/Chinese-translation-apps

Smart phones can also be used to decode the written Chinese language. Using technology known as Optical Character Recognition, or "OCR" for short, apps such as Pleco allow you to point your phone camera directly at a Chinese character and get a real-time dictionary translation.

It's important to note that using your phone as a translator often requires a connection to the internet, which means you'll need to set up your phone to be used in China.

Option #3 - Use a Tour Company

If you don't think your brain can handle attempting another language, or you just want your trip to be a relaxing experience, consider joining a tour group. It's not always the cheapest option, but at least you'll have access to a guide who can speak English and take care of all your needs. Speaking a word of Mandarin won't be necessary at all.

The good news is that you're not alone. There are plenty people who want to travel to China without speaking the language. There are day trips, 10-day trips, and longer trips available to pretty much any place that you might want to go.

The bottom line is, these companies will charge you for a pleasant trip in China, one that doesn't require you to speak Mandarin Chinese.

Learning Chinese Before You Go

Sometimes it takes a simple nudge to get each of us to try something different. Do you understand what I mean? Perhaps that's what this upcoming trip to China is for you. It's that nudge to get you to do what you've been wanting to do for a while now: learn Chinese.

Perhaps you already have a foundation of Chinese language from high school or college, but you need a good refresher. Maybe you've never learned a single word of Chinese, but you're willing to give it a shot. Whatever the case may be, you have a desire to jump into the often uncomfortable and very humbling world of language learning.

Kudos to you! I believe that learning the Chinese language not only helps make your travels go smoothly, language learning also provides a window into the culture that you won't get otherwise. The Chinese culture is already quite confusing to Westerners, and language is one of many keys that will help you to unlock the cultural insights that the Chinese language holds.

Let's take a look at some practical ways to jumpstart your Chinese language learning prior to your trip to China:

Option #1: Use a Flash Language Course

Flash language courses are an excellent solution for massive short-term language gains. I use the term "flash" because their strength lies in their ability to lay a quick foundation, not long-term fluency. If you start one of these flash courses about a month before leaving on your trip and remain diligent in your studies, you should be more than competent enough to get around China. Here is what I have personally used:

- **Pimsleur Mandarin Conversational**: I used Pimsleur before I left for China back in 2006, and I think it gave me an excellent head-start on learning the language. Why? Because in the all-audio format, it forced me to learn a Chinese accent without worrying about the characters. Pimsleur also offers a full Chinese Level 1 Course which is excellent for someone coming to live here but it would be overkill for a traveler.
- **ChinesePod**: ChinesePod is another popular option that combines a podcast-format listening experience with online learning tools. The advantage here is that there are multiple level options (beginner, intermediate, advanced) and you can choose lessons that will teach you based on your situation. This includes lessons on basic greetings, how to get around in a taxi, how to speak in a restaurant, etc.

Option #2: Online Tutoring

Online courses are useful, but they can only get you so far. There's nothing that beats full-immersion (living in China) when it comes to learning a language...but you can get close.

There are options to connect with a native Chinese tutor online, and it's surprisingly affordable. Doing a 1-on-1 tutor allows you to control the type of lessons being taught and the speed of learning.

I've personally used a service called eChineseLearning that pairs you with a Chinese tutor in China. They even offer one free lesson for first-time users. Check it out here:

www.travelchinacheaper.com/try/online-tutor

Option #3: Language Classes

There are some travelers I know who have attempted to learn Chinese by auditing a university course or taking a class at a local community college. For these people, the accountability of homework, a teacher, and classmates pushes them to learn the material better than the self-paced courses mentioned earlier. While I commend any effort to learn the Chinese language, I don't agree that this is an effective method for travelers.

There are two reasons for this. First, the Chinese method of learning, a method that is often utilized in the classroom, tends to focus on rote memorization. Repeat, repeat, repeat...and once you think you've memorized it, repeat it again. Studies have shown that this form of learning isn't as effective as contextual, spaced repetition. Second, Chinese classes at a school focus on teaching you grammar, reading, and writing. As a traveler, your focus needs to be practical language and the ability to speak.

If you need accountability, consider investing in a Chinese tutor. Explain your learning goals to your tutor, and make sure you're consistent with your meeting times.

Ordering at a Chinese Restaurant

Let's face it: whether or not you decide to learn Mandarin Chinese, you still gotta eat! For first time visitors to China, particularly those who do not speak Chinese, ordering food at a local Chinese restaurant can seem like a big challenge. A basic understanding of the dining culture and what to expect at a Chinese restaurant will go a long way in preparing for your trip.

Before we dive into how to communicate at a restaurant, I want to first paint a picture of what you should expect.

What to Expect at a Restaurant in China

Once you've chosen a restaurant, you'll sit down at the table like you would anywhere else in the world. Interestingly, that's about where the similarities end. Here's what to expect at a restaurant in China:

- **A Different Kind of Service**. Unlike Western countries, waiters at Chinese restaurants only help customers when asked for help. You will often hear locals calling out to servers using the words, "fu wu yuan" for regular staff or "lao ban" if speaking to the restaurant owner. If you are not comfortable speaking Chinese, raising your hand to get the server's attention also does the trick. I know it seems rude, but in China it's perfectly acceptable!

- **Dishes are shared and not individual.** Also, unlike Western countries where you typically order a dish for yourself, Chinese people order a number of dishes to be shared by the whole table. The only individual item you can expect is a bowl of white rice to complement your ordered dishes.
- **Chopsticks are the norm in China.** If you are not used to using chopsticks at home, start practicing in preparation for your trip. If the idea of eating with chopsticks for every meal sounds intimidating, pack yourself disposable forks and spoons to last you through your trip.
- **There is no "three-course meal" concept in China.** While it is common at proper sit-down places to order small cold dishes as an appetizer, Chinese dining does not revolve around our three-course meal concept. Order as many dishes as you like but try to finish your whole meal as ordinary Chinese do not take fondly to wasted food. For dessert, you may need to scout out a nearby bakery since watermelon or fruit is often the only dessert option at Chinese restaurants.
- **What to drink at restaurants**: Most restaurants offer generic hot tea or hot water (Chinese do not commonly drink cold beverages). Others usually have a fridge filled with an assortment of beverages like bottled water, soda, and beer. Keep in mind that there are no free refills in

China, and in most cases when you order a soft drink, it is served in a bottle or a can. Fast food restaurants like McDonald's or Burger King have fountain soda, but refills come at an additional charge.

How to Order Food at a Restaurant

Making an order at a restaurant can be a challenge, especially if you're not familiar with all the food choices. Add to that any trepidation you might have from not speaking Chinese, and it's enough to send most people packing to McDonalds!

That won't be you, though. Here are a few ways to tame that fear and order with confidence.

- **Find a restaurant with pictures on the menu**. The easiest way to order food in China is relying on menus with pictures. Simply point and use your fingers to indicate how many you want of each item, and you will be in great shape by avoiding any major language barriers while ordering.
- **Point to what looks delicious**. If there are no pictures on the menu, take a look at what other people are eating and point to what looks good as a backup way to order. Another trick is to download screenshots of common dishes you want to try in China on your phone and use those to order. It may take some body language and nod to see if those dishes are offered, but this is far easier

than staring at a menu with hundreds of options in Chinese characters.

Lastly, if you want to order in Chinese, it is best to study up on the most common dishes in preparation for your trip. To order any dish or drink, simply say, "wo yao yi ge + dish or beverage." This translates as "I want one of dish/beverage."

Paying the Bill

If you are comfortable speaking survival Chinese, use the terms, "mai dan" and "jie zhang" to ask how much you owe. However, you need a good ear for numbers as waiters typically read you the check rather than provide you a paper bill. If you can't communicate in Chinese, don't be shy to wave over the waiter and ask them to enter how much you owe on your phone calculator. It's definitely the easiest way to pay.

It's also worth noting that splitting the check isn't very common in China. This is particularly true if you're eating with a local Chinese person. It is fine for foreigners to "go Dutch," but asking a Chinese person to split the check can make the atmosphere awkward and uncomfortable. The Chinese view meals with friends as chances to build relationships or "guanxi," and they take turns treating each other to meals.

If you end up having a meal with a Chinese host, you should at least make plenty of effort to pay for the entire check. If you allow your host to cover your meal, there is the expectation that you will treat them to the next meal. This can be difficult if you are traveling and likely to move on to the next destination shortly after your meal. My suggestion when having a meal with a Chinese host is to cover it entirely. This way you are showing respect for their culture, improving your country's image abroad, and as a Westerner from a country with higher incomes than China, treating a Chinese person to a meal likely will not set you back financially.

The very last thing travelers ask about is tipping. The short answer is that there is no tipping in China. Whatever the server says you owe at the end of your meal is the total amount you need to pay. Even if you are insistent on providing a tip for good service, it will likely only result in confused looks from your waiter. The only exception to this rule is upscale restaurants that accept foreign credit cards. Often there is a space for tip, and it's considered courteous to leave one, but check to make sure they haven't already included a service gratuity.

Step 7

STAYING HEALTHY IN CHINA

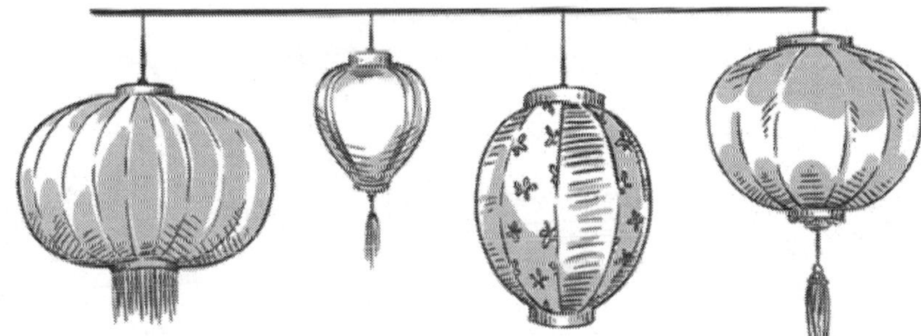

What to Expect at a Chinese Hospital

Local hospitals are a polarizing topic among expatriates living in China. I've known some foreigners who have no problem having a baby at a Chinese hospital while others wouldn't be caught dead entering a Chinese hospital. There is a wide array of opinions when it comes to healthcare in China.

In most major cities in China, there are two hospital options to choose from: the *local hospital* and the *international clinic.*

The local hospital, referred to as the 医院 or "yiyuan", is going to be your least expensive option in case of emergency. The doctors are usually well-educated, and the facilities are acceptable. On the other hand, you shouldn't expect anybody to speak fluent English at a local hospital, so it may be difficult to communicate what problem you're having. I've also had experience with many local hospitals that are overrun with patients to the point that there are three to four people sharing a room. The good news is that while your travel insurance won't be accepted at the front desk, most good insurance policies will reimburse your local hospital visit. You'll just have to front the money.

An international hospital, also known as a 国际医院 or "Guoji Yiyuan", is quite different. The facilities are usually immaculate, and the doctors are very well-educated and bilingual. Private rooms are the norm, and the whole place feels comfortable. The pricing at these hospitals is considerably higher; however, they will often accept insurance cards as payment. At the very least, they will accept international credit cards which isn't always the case with local hospitals.

I've had personal experience with both local hospitals and international hospitals in China. For most expats who call China 'home', I suggest local hospitals as a good option since expats will have a better expectation of standards. With the average traveler, however, I tend to suggest the international hospital as your first choice. Despite the added cost, it feels more familiar and is better suited to care for you.

Whichever option you choose, you've probably caught on by now that I recommend one thing to anybody who travels to China: *travel health insurance.*

Do I Need Travel Insurance?

I always tell people that insurance is a bit like counseling: it's hard to appreciate its value until you've actually had to use it.

I've had to use travel insurance before, and it was a lifesaver. My wife had suffered a traumatic injury, and we quickly rushed her to the hospital. She underwent tests, checkups, and procedures that I was sure were going to cost us thousands of dollars if not more. In the end, we paid $50.

Compare that story to the one from my friend Frank (not his real name). He was a moderately healthy 50-year old who had a stroke one day. He was rushed to a hospital where he underwent emergency surgery, and when the time came to pay...there was no money. He needed to be evacuated back to his home in the United Kingdom, but the hospital wouldn't release him until he paid his bills. These bills were getting higher and higher every single day.

In the end, his family went into debt to the tune of about US$80,000 just to get Frank out of China, back home and in good medical care. As you might imagine, Frank and his family are now big advocates of travel health insurance.

"But I'm Healthy!"

"But I'm pretty healthy," you say to yourself. *"I haven't been to a hospital in years, maybe even a decade!"* Studies show that the majority of people think they're healthy, even if they aren't. Perhaps you really are healthy, but that's not the point.

The importance of travel health insurance has little to do with whether or not you are healthy.

Travel insurance is best understood within the context of unexpected emergencies, some of which aren't even health-related. Consider the following situations:

- Your grandmother passes away and you need to cancel your trip to make the funeral. Do you forfeit all of the flight and hotel reservations?
- Your luggage gets lost when you arrive in Beijing. Are you screwed?
- You sustain a major injury that requires immediate evacuation to a hospital that can treat you well. Will you pay the $40,000+ for the air ambulance and doctors?
- You enjoy adventure activities and like to experience new thrills. Do you avoid those since most insurance companies won't cover extreme activities?

These are just a few of many examples I could give. Travel health insurance is not that expensive, and it's meant to be a safety net for those unexpected events that could ruin your trip, or worse.

Tips for Buying Travel Insurance

If you decide that travel insurance is something you should invest in (and as you can tell, I would agree with that statement), your rates and available options will depend on a number of factors including:

- Do you enjoy adventure activities that have a high degree of risk?
- Do you already have a pre-existing condition that you need covered?
- Are you over or under the age of 50?
- Will you be traveling for less than 30 days or is this longer-term travel?

Each situation might require a different kind of travel insurance. The important thing to know is that not all travel insurance cover travelers equally. You need to speak with a representative and talk with them about your specific situation. Find out what is covered by your insurance at home and then make sure that what you purchase with travel insurance covers the rest.

If you need more help choosing the right travel insurance for you, I've covered this in-depth on the TravelChinaCheaper website, which includes my own recommended insurance companies. You can find that on the following webpage.

www.travelchinacheaper.com/best-travel-insurance-guide

Traveling in China with Disabilities

For those who may be traveling to China with a disability (or perhaps even a minor handicap), I'd like to take a moment to help you understand what to expect. I would venture a guess that over 90% of China is not equipped to handle even the most basic of disabilities: braille is not common, ramps are rare, handrails are unheard of.

Frankly speaking, if you are confined to a wheelchair or have difficulty walking, you're going to find China a challenge. Sidewalks are uneven and fraught with obstacles and potholes. I don't know if I've ever seen a public bus that accommodates wheelchairs, although I know they exist.

Mind you, Chinese people are extremely respectful and helpful to the elderly and disabled. I've seen people go out of their way to help somebody in a wheelchair successfully board a bus. The issue isn't people; it's infrastructure.

China is making great strides in accommodating those with disabilities, particularly at major tourist spots, but it still has a long, long way to go. It's quite possible that you're going to have difficulty getting down the steps in front of your hotel but find yourself completely taken care of while visiting The Great Wall. Nothing surprises me anymore.

Frequently Asked Questions

I receive a number of emails each day from travelers like you who are planning their trip to China. They've asked me hundreds of different questions, most of which I've answered in the chapters in this book. There are a few questions, however, that don't really fit within the outline of this guide, so I'd like to answer them here.

What Parts of China Require a Permit to Travel?

Ninety percent of China is completely open to travelers as long as you have a proper Chinese visa. There are a few places, however, where a special permit is required. These places include Tibet, which requires travelers to join a travel group, and border areas along the Xinjiang region. If you're headed to any politically sensitive areas such as these, you'll want to connect with a local travel agency to determine what, if any, permits are needed.

Can I Bring my Drone to Fly in China?

Yes, personal drones can be flown in China as long as you're flying outside of what is known as the "No Fly Zone". China requires that you register your drone prior to flying and follow all drone laws. This is entirely your responsibility. You won't be questioned at the airport about your drone, but there is a chance that you'll be asked for registration. I've never been asked, but I know others who have. To learn more about the specific laws governing drones and how to register your drone, check out the following webpage:

www.travelchinacheaper.com/china-drones

Should I Give Gifts to my China Hosts?

If you're planning to visit a friend in China or be hosted by a local, it's important that you don't arrive empty-handed. Gift giving is an important part of Chinese culture, and while it doesn't have to be expensive, it is a way to solidify the relationship. No matter if it's a business relationship, family relationship, or just a friendship, save some room in your suitcase to bring a snack or special item from your home country.

Do I Need to Bring a Pollution Mask?

You've probably heard a lot about China's bad pollution, and much of what you've heard is unfortunately true. Thankfully, China is making great strides to clean its air, but it's still going to take time for these policy changes to take effect. Face masks are easy to purchase and are very cheap here in China, so if it's absolutely necessary to have one, you'll be able to find one. In general, you'll have to worry about pollution more during the winter months than in the summer months.

Can You Help Me Find a Chinese Wife?

No, I'm sorry. I can't do that. Seriously, though...I get that question more than you'd imagine!

****

If you have additional questions that haven't been answered, I invite you to join a community of China travelers I host on Facebook. Most questions get answered in just a couple hours.

www.facebook.com/groups/chinatravelcommunity

Preparation Complete - Now Go!

We've now covered a lot of ground in preparation for your trip to China. I hope you feel better prepared and most importantly, that your expectations have been set correctly!

Now I encourage you to go. Don't put it off! Take the plunge and book your travel. Explore a part of the world that you have never seen before.

As Mark Twain so eloquently said:

> *"Twenty years from now you will be more disappointed by the things that you didn't do than by the ones you did do. So throw off the bowlines. Sail away from the safe harbor. Catch the trade winds in your sails. Explore. Dream. Discover."*

APPENDIX

Travel Packing List

While working with hundreds of travelers planning their trips to China, I've come to realize how valuable it is to know what is and isn't available for purchase at local stores. This helps to know what is important to bring with you in your luggage and what can be purchased when you arrive.

Below is a simple list of items that you should consider packing and tasks you should do before you leave. If you'd like to have a printable packing list, I've created a free one that you can download on the book bonuses page here:

www.travelchinacheaper.com/book-bonuses

Travel Preparation Checklist

- ✓ Check Your Passport. Check that your passport has at least six months of validity in addition to your China visa.
- ✓ Make a copy of your passport and visa pages: It's best if these are kept in a different suitcase.
- ✓ Purchase Airline Tickets: I also suggest that you print out your itinerary to carry with you.

- ✓ Buy a China travel guide
- ✓ Notify your bank of upcoming travel dates: Do this so that they don't freeze your account while pulling money from an international ATM!
- ✓ Purchase a VPN: As has already been covered in the chapter about Censorship & the Internet in China, if you want access to your regular social media, email, and streaming content, you're going to want to buy a VPN prior to your departure. I recommend ExpressVPN.
- ✓ Put Your Mail on Hold: If you'll be gone for longer than a week (which is probably the case for a trip to China), make sure to let the post office know so your mail doesn't stack up. At the very least, have a friend or neighbor pick up your mail while you're gone.
- ✓ Arrange for Airport Pickup/Dropoff
- ✓ Purchase Travel Insurance

Clothing Checklist

- ✓ Underwear: Preferably you'll want some quick-dry underwear that you can wash and dry easily.
- ✓ Socks: You can buy these in China, but it's best to bring your own.
- ✓ Comfortable Hiking/Walking Shoes: You'll be walking a lot in China, so make sure you have comfortable shoes!
- ✓ Rain Jacket: I recommend this even during the summer. There are very light and packable jackets you can buy.

- ✓ Shorts
- ✓ Hiking Pants: In my opinion, jeans are often too heavy for packing.
- ✓ Sunglasses
- ✓ Shirts
- ✓ At least one "business casual" outfit: I add this in case you end up going to a nicer restaurant or event.
- ✓ Earplugs and/or Eye mask: These are useful when traveling to and around China.

Electronics Checklist

- ✓ Extra Camera Batteries and Memory Cards: That is unless the only camera you're using is your phone.
- ✓ China Plug Converter: Make sure you have the right plug and/or power converter.
- ✓ Camera & Phone Chargers: You can buy charging cables cheaply in China, but it's best to bring your own.
- ✓ Headphones
- ✓ Tablet with plenty of good books

Medicine / First Aid Checklist

- ✓ Pepto Bismol Chewables: There's a good chance you'll need these!

- ✓ Aspirin: Useful if you're prone to headaches. It's available at a China pharmacy but easier to just bring it yourself.
- ✓ Prescription Meds: Don't leave them at home...they're hard to find here in China.
- ✓ Dramamine: Useful if you're prone to motion sickness.

Toiletries Checklist

- ✓ Toothbrush/Toothpaste
- ✓ Deodorant: This isn't easy to purchase in China.
- ✓ Soap and Shampoo: This is available in hotels but not always in hostels.
- ✓ Bug Spray: This is for mosquitos if you're traveling outside the big cities.
- ✓ Sunscreen: You won't find good sunscreen in China, and in many places you'll need it.
- ✓ Quick-Dry Towel: If you won't be staying at hotels, these towels are invaluable while staying at hostels.
- ✓ Tampons: Pads are easy to find in China, but tampons are still a challenge to buy.
- ✓ Hand Sanitizer: Not every bathroom in China has soap, so you'll want to bring your own.

Recommended Travel Operators

When it comes to tour operators, I have a personal motto that I follow when traveling: *"Travel globally; tour locally."*

What this means is that while I love to visit new places all over the globe, I prefer to give my business to local tour operators instead of country-wide travel agencies. There are a couple reasons for this. First, if I'm going to pay for a tour, I want my money to have the greatest impact on the local economy. This isn't always the case whenever the branch offices of a large travel agency send half their earnings back to the headquarters in another part of the country.

Second, and more importantly, I believe that a local tour operator (both Chinese and foreign) is usually going to provide you with a more authentic experience. They know where the best restaurants are. They can often set up a home visit or a food tour. They do more than just bus you to the next tourist destination.

Perhaps you've already booked your tour with an agency you found online. Maybe you're already connected with China's CITS (China International Travel Service), the largest travel agency in China. If that's you, don't worry! My goal isn't to criticize any particular travel agency; my goal is to promote local agencies where possible. If you're in the market for a good tour in one of the places listed below, check one of these places out. I think you'll be glad you did!

Beijing

- **Beijing Walking Tours**: You can walk through the Forbidden City...or you can have an historian and excellent storyteller like Jeremiah Jenne help you visualize the history of the place. Jeremiah and his team present Chinese history in such an entertaining way. They offer scheduled tours at all the major Beijing destinations as well as private and custom tours.

www.beijingbyfoot.com

Shanghai

- **Jenny's Shanghai Tours**: Jenny and her team of local guides are some of the best in Shanghai. They provide friendly, English-speaking guides and offer a number of excellent walking tours, history tours and food tour options.

www.jennysshanghaitours.com

Xi'an (Shaanxi)

- **China Xi'an Tour:** With more than 15 years of experience in Xi'an, this local agency offers more than the typical Xi'an tour. They have food tours, Muslim quarter tours, "local experience" tours, night tours and they can even help arrange car rentals.

www.chinaxiantour.com

Chengdu (Sichuan)

- **Chengdu Food Tours**: Sichuan cuisine is world-famous, and there's no better place to try it for yourself than when you're in Chengdu. Instead of trying a random restaurant and guessing what's good on the menu, join a CFT group to visit the restaurants that are famous among the locals and try the food that you wouldn't know to order yourself!

www.chengdufoodtours.com

Yunan

- **Yunnan Adventure Travel:** This local agency has been specializing in travel around Yunnan for over a decade. You'll find the classic Yunnan tours here (visiting the Leaping Gorge, Shangri-La, LiJiang, etc.) as well as some interesting wildlife and outdoor adventure tours.

www.yunnanadventure.com

Hong Kong

- **AnyTours:** This Hong Kong-based travel agency offers a number of great local options including helicopter rides, evening ferries on the harbor, historic tours and of course help with a visit to Disney World.

www.anytours.com.hk

Tibet

- **Tibetan Guide**: Led by a local Tibetan named Mima Dhondup and based in the capital of Lhasa, Tibetan Guide is one of the best options for those who wish to travel the Tibetan plateau. You can call or email to inquire about tours; they are extremely responsive.

www.tibetanguide.com

Xinjiang

- **Old Road Tours**: Based in the Silk Road oasis of Kashgar, Old Road Tours is run by a Uyghur family that has been helping foreign travelers for over a decade. I know them personally, and they do great work all across the Xinjiang region.

www.oldroadtours.com

- **FarWestChina**: Not to toot my own horn, but if you're traveling to Xinjiang, you'll want to purchase the comprehensive Xinjiang travel guide I published through FarWestChina. It's one of the only (and therefore one of the best) travel guides on the market. I'll even give you 30 percent off when you use the code TCC30 at checkout!

www.xjtravelguide.com

China-Wide Tour Operators

If you truly need a travel agency that can help you book an entire trip across the whole of China, I recommend you get quotes from the following places:

- **Wendy Wu Tours:** Great tour options for those travelers from the UK, Ireland, Australia, New Zealand and South Africa.

  www.wendywutours.com

- **China Highlights:** Choose from a long list of tour options or have one custom-designed for your group. A good option for those travelers from the USA, Canada, and the rest of Europe.

  www.chinahighlights.com

Suggested Reading

There are literally thousands of books written about China and not every one of them fits the needs and tastes of each traveler. For this reason, I'd like to offer suggestions on reading material that I've found useful. Each of the books listed below can be purchased as a physical book or Kindle e-book.

Books on Chinese History

I'm a huge believer in the value of understanding contextual history wherever I travel. It gives me a greater appreciation for any place I visit and helps me be a more educated traveler. Honestly, it's almost impossible to synthesize thousands of years of history into one book. Even still, I'd like to suggest a few books (and an audiobook) that do a good job:

- The Rise and Fall of China (Audiobook): For those who would appreciate an audiobook to listen to while running or doing errands (or on a plane flying to China), I love *Audible*. Although this "book" is technically a university course, it listens like a novel. It's an entertaining and very educational look at modern

Chinese history. Best of all, if you're not already subscribed to *Audible*, they offer one audiobook for free.

- The Rape of Nanking: If you ask any Chinese person about the most influential event in China's modern history, most will talk of China's struggle against Japan. Even today, more than a generation removed from World War II, young Chinese people are still trained to despise Japan. This difficult but true story gives the background of why this animosity exists and how it has shaped modern China.
- On China: Written by former Secretary of State Henry Kissinger, the book *On China* tells the story of China's modern history in relation to both the US and the USSR. Kissinger brings a unique and informed perspective on China that is fascinating and compelling.
- Understanding China: A Guide to China's Economy, History, and Political Culture Written by Yale University lecturer John Bryan Starr, this book is a great introduction and overview of China's history and economy. There are a number of great maps and statistical graphs that present information in a helpful visual format.

Books on Chinese Culture

If history books come across as too "dry" for you, perhaps you'll enjoy some of these more entertaining books on modern

Chinese culture. These books blend personal stories with insightful analysis of modern China.

- Oracle Bones: Among writers about China, Peter Hessler is considered one of the best. A former Peace Corp volunteer, Hessler has written a number of books which tell the story of China in a most entertaining way. *Oracle Bones* is one of the best, but I urge you to look at his other titles including *River Town* and *Country Driving*.
- Street of Eternal Happiness: Big City Dreams Along a Shanghai Road Another ex-Peace Corp teacher and current National Public Radio (NPR) correspondent, Rob Schmitz does an excellent job telling the story of Shanghai's modern history and culture through the eyes of various characters along a single city street.
- Age of Ambition: Chasing Fortune, Truth, and Faith in the New China Written by Evan Osnos, who was the China correspondent for *The New Yorker* from 2008 to 2013, *Age of Ambition* is an excellent read that has won numerous awards. Osnos has a special way of capturing the essence of China's culture and diversity that makes me nod my head and laugh at the same time.
- Wish Lanterns: Young Lives in New China In Wish Lanterns, my friend and author Alec Ash follows the stories of six young Chinese youth from different parts of China. It's a fascinating look at how different parts of China have produced significantly diverse worldviews.

Special Discounts

Having worked in the China travel industry for years, I've developed relationships with a number of great companies that I use and trust. As a thank you for purchasing this guide, I've been able to leverage these relationships to negotiate special discounts for you. You probably won't have a need for all these services, but hopefully some of them will come in handy.

Also, I think it's important for me to share with you two things here.

First, I have used each of these services for years, not just weeks or months. I wouldn't recommend them if I wasn't a happy customer myself.

Second, these links are known as "affiliate links" which means that at no extra cost to you, I will be compensated if you decide to use these services. You are under no obligation to use these links, but your support helps me to continue providing great travel content like this. Thank you!

China Visa Services

- **Passport Visa Express**: Use the code TCC10 in order to get 10% off your visa processing fees. Please note that this is only good for US residents and you must use this link in order for that code to work.

www.travelchinacheaper.com/try/pve

VPN Services

- **ExpressVPN**: I use a VPN every day in China to get around censorship of sites like Facebook, Gmail, Instagram, YouTube, Netflix and others. When you use this link to purchase an annual subscription (which I recommend in order to protect you online even when you're not traveling), ExpressVPN will give you three months of free service on top of the 12-month plan.

www.travelchinacheaper.com/view/expressvpn

- **NordVPN**: As an alternative – or as I recommend to any serious traveler as a "backup," NordVPN is an excellent, easy to use VPN service. If you absolutely must have internet access without any censorship, it's advisable to have at least one backup VPN in case your primary service gets blocked.

www.travelchinacheaper.com/ebook/nordvpn

Chinese Language Learning

- **ChinesePod**: I've loved using ChinesePod to learn Chinese! It's a service that offers podcasts, video lessons, and so much more. You can try the program for one month free and get a $50 discount on the annual package when you use the code TCCHINA.

  www.travelchinacheaper.com/try/chinesepod

- **eChineseLearning**: For an even faster way to improve your Chinese, nothing beats one-on-one tutoring. It's now possible to do this online with a native speaker thanks to services like eChineseLearning. You can try your first tutor lesson for free using the following link.

www.travelchinacheaper.com/try/echineselearning-trial

Traveler's Mail Service

- **Traveling Mailbox**: If you travel a lot and would like to have access to your physical mail while you're away, or perhaps you're a business owner who needs a registered address, I've used Traveling Mailbox for the past few years, and it's been great. They scan a copy of my mail when it comes in, which then gets sent to either my phone or email. I can tell them to open, scan, forward, shred...whatever I need. You can get two months of free service by using this link:

  www.travelchinacheaper.com/try/travel-mail

Made in the USA
Lexington, KY
14 September 2019